Simply Bonaventure

Simply Bonaventure

An Introduction to His Life, Thought, and Writings

Ilia Delio, O.S.F.

New City Press

Published in the United States by New City Press
202 Cardinal Rd., Hyde Park, NY 12538
www.newcitypress.com

Cover design by Nick Cianfarani

Library of Congress Cataloging-in-Publication Data:
Delio, Ilia.
Simply Bonaventure : an introduction to his life, thought, and writings / by Ilia Delio.
p. cm.
Includes bibliographical references and index.
ISBN 1-56548-161-5
1. Bonaventure, Saint, Cardinal, ca. 1217-1274 I. Title

B765.B74 D45 2001
230'.2'092--dc21 2001037001
[B]

Printed in Canada

In loving memory of my father
who has returned to God

Contents

Bonaventure's Life

Bonaventure's Thought

Excerpts of Bonaventure's Writings

Acknowledgments

A book is born of an idea but nurtured through conversation and friendship with others. My first debt of gratitude is to Professor Ewert Cousins of Fordham University who originally drafted a book entitled *The Essential Bonaventure* and who passed on the unfinished manuscript to me. As always, his encouragement and support continue to be a source of inspiration. I am also indebted to Eleanor Granger, O.S.F., Patricia Reed and Devote Ryan for their careful reading of the text and helpful comments. A special thanks is due to Daniel Grigassy, O.F.M., and Stephen Kluge, O.F.M., for helping me to get the text into its final shape. With a few dinners at Mark's Kitchen and some critical reading, grammatical errors were eliminated and complex points of Bonaventure's theology were clarified. After reading the book, Steve graciously offered to contribute his own spiritual reflections which are included at the end of each chapter. I would also like to thank my colleague Dominic Monti, O.F.M., as well as Dr. Timothy Johnson, for offering their expertise in reviewing several difficult parts of Bonaventure's first collation on the *Hexaëmeron*.

I undertook this project as part of my sabbatical at the Washington Theological Union. Anticipating the onerous task of research and writing, I soon found myself caught up in the deep intertwining of theology and spirituality that is unique to Bonaventure. What began as work, therefore, was transformed into a spiritual journey. Bonaventure became my spiritual guide and my sabbatical became a retreat on the journey to God. It is my hope that all those who read *Simply Bonaventure* will also embark on this wonderful journey, for Bonaventure gets to the heart of what it means to be truly human and loved by God.

Introduction

Approximately seven years ago I was standing in the office of Ewert Cousins at Fordham University. Anyone who has visited Professor Cousin's office is immediately struck by the periphery of books, dissertations and papers lining the walls. At one point, Ewert climbed over a pile of books and reached into his filing cabinet pulling out a manuscript that he had worked on but never completed. He handed it to me and I was impressed by the title, "The Essential Bonaventure." Since that time I have mulled over the idea of "The Essential Bonaventure" hoping one day that I could complete the manuscript.

The present book, *Simply Bonaventure*, is an offshoot of that initial idea. It is somewhat different in structure and scope from that which Professor Cousins had originally intended. My reasons for this book are several. First, the growing interest in Bonaventure's theology today among a variety of people calls for a less technical and more general approach to his theology. Bonaventure's scholastic "style," his language, rich with symbolism and the numerical patterning of his ideas, all make for difficult reading to the untrained eye. The complex medieval thought patterns that characterize Bonaventure's writings can be either intimidating and, or, frustrating, and the question is often asked, "what is he *really* saying?" Despite the difficulties of his writings, Bonaventure's theological system is a profound and unique synthesis complete with its own metaphysics, and can provide a meaningful substrate to contemporary Christian life. In order to open the doors of his theology to others, however, it must become "user friendly." This book is written as an invitation to enter into his world.

Although it is somewhat presumptuous to call this book *Simply Bonaventure* in light of the complexity of Bonaventure's thought, I believe the *essence* of his thought is contained in a simple formula that Bonaventure himself professed: "This is our entire metaphysics: emanation, exemplarity, and consummation, that is, to be illumined by rays of spiritual light and to return to the Most High."[1] Translating this into more contemporary terms Bonaventure was ultimately concerned with three questions: 1) Where have we come from? 2) What are we doing here? 3) Where are we going? Rather than approaching these as open-ended questions, however, Bonaventure began with the conviction of faith in God who has revealed himself to us in Jesus Christ. "Unless we are able to view things in terms of how they originate, how they are to be reduced to their end, and how God shines forth in them, we will not be able to understand."[2] Always searching for the ultimate ground of truth, he came to perceive the fullness of truth in Jesus Christ. Thus, he indicated, if we want to know the ground of our being, the purpose of our existence and the goal to which we are directed, we must come to know Christ who is the center of our lives and our universe.

To explore the world of this profound theologian, I have divided the book into three main sections: Bonaventure's life, thought, and writings. With regard to his life, there is little that can be said. Although Bonaventure was a major public figure for most of his life, the lack of an official biography or unbiased eyewitness account(s) of his life makes it difficult to construct an accurate portrait of this theologian and saint. However, it is reasonable to say that something of the person shines through in his writings. Thus, as more of Bonaventure's writings come to the fore, so too does this mystic and leader become more readily "visible."

The area I have concentrated on in this book is Bonaventure's thought. I place the emphasis on *thought* rather than *theology* or *writings* because my attempt here is to answer the question, "what is Bonaventure *really* saying?" Etienne Gilson once remarked that Bonaventure's theology is of such remarkable harmony and unity that one either sees the whole or one sees nothing at all. No one part can be extracted in isolation from the whole.[3] In light of Gilson's remark, I have attempted an overall synthesis of Bonaventure's thought based on his own metaphysical structure of emanation, exemplarity, and consummation.

The pattern of Bonaventure's thought is "circular"—we come from God, we exist in relation to God and we are to return to God.[4] The basis of this "circle" is the Trinity in which the Father who is the fountain-fullness of goodness communicates goodness to the Son who, in turn, loves the Father in the Spirit. For Bonaventure, God is an infinite primordial mystery of self-communicative love. Just as the Father is the source and goal of the immanent emanations of the Trinity, so too the Father is the source and goal of all created reality. Thus, everything flows from the Father (*emanation*) and ultimately returns to the Father (*consummation*). Bonaventure frequently used the image of water to describe the God of overflowing love as a vast and living fountain of water.[5] As Zachary Hayes writes:

> Flowing from that fountain as something willed and loved by God is the immense river of creation. The world of nature is a vast expression of a loving will. Such a world is not one-dimensional, but like water, it has many qualities and dimensions. Like the water of the ocean, the world has an overwhelming fullness as it flows from the depths of God. Like the ocean, it is deep and contains many levels of meaning. Like the water of a river, the world flows in such fluidity and richness that it cannot be contained in any one form or category. And as—according to *Ecclesiastes* 1:7—rivers return to their place of origin, so the river of creation circles back on its place of origin. Emanation is simultaneously a movement toward the return or reduction of creation to God. Created existence, therefore, is a dynamic reality, directed in its inner core to a fulfillment and completion which is to be the mysterious fruit of its history.[6]

The image of life as a flowing fountain or stream emanating from the mouth of God imparts a dynamic image to God and creation. For Bonaventure, God is not the disinterested unmoved mover who has nothing in common with creation. Rather, God is the infinite dynamic fountain-fullness of self-communicative love who, by the very nature of being love, is at once Most High and intimately related to us (*altissime et piissime*).[7] God is the source of our lives and the goal to which we are directed. With this in mind, I have arranged the chapters so that they follow the pattern of emanation, exemplarity and consummation (reduction). Since the basis of emanation is the Trinity I begin with the mystery of divine, infinite, self-diffusive goodness that undergirds the Trinity. By understanding the Trinity and the relationships of the divine persons we come to a more profound understanding of creation and, within creation, humanity. The Trinity provides a "blueprint" for creation since the relationship between the Father and Son/Word, united in the Spirit, is the ground of all other relationships. The triad of Trinity—creation—humanity manifests the dynamism of God's self-communicative love whereby creation and humanity spiral forth from the overflowing goodness of God.

The question of why we exist finds meaning on three different but interrelated levels: first, in the mirror of creation, second, in the creation of the human person as image of God and, ultimately, in the Incarnation. Bonaventure offers a rich anthropology that is grounded in a cosmic Christology. His theology of Incarnation is much closer to the cosmic Christology of the Greek Fathers than to Anselm's doctrine of satisfaction, and he highlights the Incarnation as both a work of redemption and cosmic completion. Understanding the primary reason for the Incarnation in terms of cosmic completion reflects the profound role the human person has in creation, since the human person alone is created in a particular way, congruent to the Word of God. The human person, therefore, is structured to the mystery of Christ who is the divine-temporal exemplar. Bonaventure places a special emphasis on devotion to the humanity of Christ whereby imitation of Christ is integral to the journey to God. Through imitation of Christ, the human person participates in the building up of the body of Christ which in Bonaventure's view undergirds the reduction or leading back of all things to God. The chapters on Incarnation, Soul's Journey and Imitation of Christ, therefore, form a second triad whereby conformity to Christ leads one into the heart of God. It is in union with Christ that one arrives at true contemplation which may be described as a transcendence in love. At this final stage of the journey, one enters into the mystery of the Father whereby silence and love prevail. Bonaventure sees the fruits of contemplation—wisdom, peace and ecstatic love—manifested in the desire for martyrdom which, in his view, can usher in the final age of historical peace. Thus, the last few chapters of this section explore the centrality of Christ in the Christian life, the road to contemplation and the attainment of peace.

The final chapter, "Reductio," explores how and why all things must lead back to God. The key to reduction according to Bonaventure lies in the human person created in the image of God. In a sense the new birth of creation and the destiny of history are contingent on the freedom of the human person. Bonaventure realized that while all things come from God and in some way reflect God, it is the human person alone who is created in the divine image and can attain a true relationship with God. The capacity of the human person for God, however, is not a matter for the individual alone. In Bonaventure's view, one's relationship with God influences the destiny of creation and the consummation of history. Our lives not only make a difference but a cosmic difference. While the human person is capable of knowing and loving God, such a capacity is grounded in freedom. God has revealed the way, the truth and the life in Christ but we must have the desire to see. For Bonaventure, the light to see is already within us but we must turn toward this light, and the very act of turning is itself a decision made in freedom and in response to grace.

Although Bonaventure's thought must be explored from the point of theology, I have tried at the same time to highlight the relevancy of his thought for contemporary Christian life. It is perhaps a methodological error to extract a medieval theologian's ideas and apply them to the twenty-first century; however, I am not strictly "splicing and inserting." While I am aware that Bonaventure's Ptolemaic universe was vastly different from our evolutionary one, I am also fairly certain that humanity has not changed in the last eight hundred years. The essential questions that Bonaventure raised in the thirteenth century are still relevant to us in the twenty-first century, namely, What is our origin? What is our purpose? And to where are we going? Perhaps, most importantly as Christians in a global world, the critical question for us today concerns the meaning and purpose of Jesus Christ. While Bonaventure's theology does not provide immediate answers, his metaphysical system with Christ as center provides a rich integral synthesis of God, humanity and creation that can impart vital meaning and hope to contemporary Christian life.

The last section is a brief introduction to Bonaventure's writings. Excerpts from the writings reveal the voices he assumed throughout his lifetime: theologian-scholar, leader-pastor, defender of the faith. The strictly theological works are formal scholastic treatments of theological questions written at the University of Paris and are more objective and "scientific" in nature. Bonaventure's spiritual writings, including his more prescriptive writings, were composed during his tenure as Minister General of the Franciscan Order and reflect his various roles as brother-friar, seeker of God, spiritual director and religious leader. These writings, in particular, disclose Bonaventure's mystical spirit and his passionate love of God revealed in Christ crucified in whom he saw the mystery of God and creation united. A final series of works known as "lectures" (*collationes*) complete the corpus of Bonaventure's works. These were delivered to the faculty and students at the University of Paris at a time when Latin Aristotelianism was threatening to uproot Christian doctrine.

Bonaventure's lectures stand firm on the conviction of faith in Jesus Christ and reinforce the primacy of theology in the face of philosophical inquiry. Taken in concert, Bonaventure's writings (and we might add the staggering number of these works) reveal a fertile mind, a passionate heart, a generous spirit and a consuming passion for truth.

Despite his demanding role as Minister General of the Franciscan Order for almost a third of his life, Bonaventure maintained a steady gaze on the mystery of God revealed in Christ and him crucified. Whether at the University, in the friary, in the pulpit or in the parlor of the Poor Clare nuns, Bonaventure never ceased to pursue the questions of origin, purpose and destiny. In his view, unless we know where we come from we cannot return. In our age where meaning and purpose of human existence is becoming increasingly vague, and the quest for human identity shows the mark of desperation, Bonaventure offers a profound system of thought that can help redefine the boundaries of what it means to be human and Christian. It is, indeed, a search and a journey that begins with desire and prayer and spirals through the complexities of our lives, as we seek to find God at the center of our existence. Bonaventure reassures us that on this journey God is not only with us but in us, leading us in light despite the sense of ever present darkness. To recognize God within us is to let go in freedom—of clinging to that which is not God—and to embrace in love that which is God even in the midst of suffering humanity. In the end, we cannot understand the mystery of God within us and in our world; we can only yield to this mystery in love. Then, and only then, however, do we see the face of God and live, for to yield in love is to return to the point from which we began. And in this return we discover the truth of who we are created to be and the truth of the world in all its beauty.

Ilia Delio, O.S.F.

Notes

1. Bonaventure, *Collationes in Hexaëmeron* (hereafter *Hex.*) 1.17 (V, 332). "[Hoc est medium *metaphysicum* reducens], et haec est tota nostra metaphysica: de emanatione, de exemplaritate, de consummatione, scilicet illuminari per radios spirituales et reduci ad summum." All Bonaventure's works cited in this volume are from the critical edition, *Doctoris Seraphici S. Bonaventurase opera omnia.* 10 Volumes, in folio. (Ad Claras Aquas, Quaracchi: Collegium S. Bonaventurae, 1882–1902). Latin texts are indicated by volume and page number in parentheses.

2. *Hex.* 3.2 (V, 343). "Nisi enim quis possit considerare de rebus, qualiter originantur, qualiter in finem reducuntur, et qualiter in eis refulget Deus; intelligientiam habere non potest."

3. Etienne Gilson, *The Philosophy of Saint Bonaventure*, trans. Illtyd Trethowan and F. J. Sheed (New York: Sheed and Ward, 1938), 430.

4. Although the idea of a metaphysical circle is a Hellenistic concept which underscores an eternal world, Bonaventure did not appropriate the image of the circle in this manner. Rather, he describes the "circle of life" within the linear direction of history. The circle expresses a Christian concept of creation as a temporal-historical reality. Because God, who is creator, creates out of nothing (*ex nihilo*), the world has a definite beginning (from God) and end in which everything attains its final consummation in God. As he states in his disputed questions on evangelical perfection: "Omega revolvit ad alpha." See Bonaventure, *Questiones disputatae de perfectione evangelica* (hereafter *Perf. ev.*) q. 2, a. 2.20 (V, 148).

5. Bonaventure, I *Commentarius in Libros Sententiarum* (hereafter *Sent.*) prooem. (I, 1–6); idem, *Breviloquium* (hereafter *Brev.*) prol. 1 (V, 203).

6. Zachary Hayes, *The Hidden Center: Spirituality and Speculative Christology in St. Bonaventure* (St. Bonaventure, NY: The Franciscan Institute, 1992), 13.

7. *Brev.* 1.2 (V, 211).

Bonaventure's Life

From Paris to Assisi

Around 1235, a young man by the name of Giovanni di Fidanza entered the University of Paris. Barely eighteen years old, Giovanni began his studies for the master of arts degree.[1] In time, this young man would assume the leadership of one of the fastest-growing religious movements in medieval Europe—the Franciscans—and would be recognized as one of the leading General Ministers of the Order. He would eventually be known as Bonaventure of Bagnoregio.

Paris was the place to be in the thirteenth century if one was intent on studying theology. Filled with the currents of a new cosmic consciousness spilling over from the writings of the Pseudo-Dionysius, Augustine, and new translations of Plato and Aristotle, Paris was the hub of intellectual life. And with the rise of scholasticism, thanks to the genius of Peter Abelard and the *Sentences* of Peter Lombard, theology was quickly becoming a scientific discipline as much as it had been an experiential one—at least within the walls of the cloister.[2]

Bonaventure began his studies under one of Europe's leading theologians, Alexander of Hales. An Englishman by birth, Alexander held the chair in theology at Paris and soon came in contact with a group of poor mendicants known as Franciscans. Inspired by their simplicity, poverty and gospel way of life, Alexander decided to join the Franciscans in 1236 at the age of fifty.[3] This marked a turning point for the Franciscans, for upon joining the Order, Alexander not only continued to teach but he brought his chair of theology with him, establishing the school of the Friars Minor as an official part of the University of Paris. Although Bonaventure had several influential Franciscan teachers, John of La Rochelle, Eudes Rigaud and William of Middleton, for example, it is most likely that the striking example of Alexander of Hales influenced Bonaventure to join the Franciscans in 1243. In a letter to an unknown university Master, Bonaventure confesses that he was attracted to the Franciscans by the simplicity and learning of the scholars at Paris. The example of these scholars, in his view, reflected the primitive church. He wrote:

> For I confess before God that what made me love Saint Francis's way of life so much was that it is exactly like the origin and the perfection of the Church itself, which began first with simple fishermen and afterward developed to include the most illustrious and learned doctors. You find the same thing in the Order of Saint Francis; in this way God reveals that it did not come about through human calculations but through Christ.[4]

The relationship between master and student was an important one, for Bonaventure received from Alexander the substance of the tradition that would shape his own synthesis—especially the currents flowing from Augustine, the Pseudo-Dionysius and the Victorines.[5] Bonaventure considered himself a disciple of Alexander, referring to him as his "father" and "master" and, in turn, Alexander deeply admired and respected Bonaventure, saying "that it seemed as though Adam had not sinned in him."[6]

After Alexander's death, Bonaventure continued to study under Eudes Rigaud and William of Middleton. In 1248 he was licensed as a bachelor of Scripture and for the next two years lectured on the Bible. From 1250 to 1252, he lectured on the *Sentences* of Peter Lombard which formed the basis of theology in the Middle Ages. In 1252 and 1253 he was engaged in disputations and preaching. In 1253 or 1254 he was awarded the licentiate and doctorate which gave him the right to teach not only at Paris but throughout Christendom.[7] As he progressed through these various degrees, he produced a number of writings: commentaries on the four books of the

Sentences; commentaries on the Gospels of Luke and John, as well as the book of Ecclesiastes; disputed questions on the knowledge of Christ, the Trinity, and Evangelical Perfection; and a most original work for its time, a "summa" of theology known as the *Breviloquium*. Throughout these works, the seed of Bonaventure's thought took root and would later reach maturity in his lectures and spiritual writings.

During the last few years of his tenure at the University of Paris (of more than twenty years), Bonaventure was caught up in one of the most vicious disputes regarding the number of chairs in the theology faculty. The dispute was between the secular masters and the mendicant orders. The secular masters resented the invasion of the mendicants into positions of authority and power which the faculty chairs conceded. Such mendicants, William of St. Amour claimed, were false prophets and their way of life was contrary to morality and religion. Bonaventure, now regent Master of the Franciscan school, took up the friars' defense, justifying the mendicant status of the Order and its particular role in the Church.[8] Bonaventure's work, *Disputed Questions on Evangelical Perfection,* not only established him as one of the outstanding theologians of his day[9] but would remain an important work for Franciscans throughout history.

As the feud between the secular masters and mendicants continued at Paris, the Franciscan Order itself, having grown from a few thousand friars in Francis's time to over 30,000 friars by 1250 (twenty-four years after Francis's death), was experiencing conflict and division that threatened survival of the Order. The principal source of conflict emerged from a factious group of Franciscans known as the zealots (*zelanti*). Enamored by the teachings of the Calabrian abbot, Joachim of Fiore, the Franciscan zealots were committed to strict poverty, purity, simplicity and ascetic piety.[10] They not only rejected learning and organizational structure within the Order, but some held to a radical Joachitism and prophesied that an age of the Spirit would supplant the present ecclesiastical structures. With this new age, they claimed, would come a new and eternal Gospel, thus superceding the New Testament itself. Francis of Assisi, they maintained, was the herald of this new age. As the angel of the sixth seal who had ushered in the new age of the Spirit, the life of Francis marked the final age of this world.

There is really no historical evidence to indicate how Bonaventure reacted when the Minister General, John of Parma, resigned from his position at the chapter of Aracoeli in Rome, February 2, 1257.[11] The reasons for John's resignation are not entirely certain but may have been due in part to his affiliation with the zealots and his sympathy for radical Joachitism.[12] While John's resignation must have been startling, the real shock came in John's suggestion to the chapter that Bonaventure succeed him as Minister General saying: "he knew not a better man in the Order."[13] The members of the chapter agreed and, in 1257, Bonaventure was elected the seventh Minister General of the Order of Friars Minor. Trained as a theologian, enjoying a successful teaching career, Bonaventure relinquished his position at the University to assume the responsibilities of Minister General in an Order that was on the brink of chaos.[14]

It is the fate of history and the hand of God that changed Bonaventure's life so radically and, we might say, the Order itself, for Bonaventure proved to be not only a successful theologian but an able administrator, introducing norms and procedures that would consolidate the diverse factions of friars. In the ensuing years, Bonaventure traveled extensively throughout Europe, including Italy, Spain, France, Germany and perhaps England, to meet with communities of friars. The exhaustive nature of these travels is apparent when one considers the time involved. Although the combination of roads and ferry services would have offered Bonaventure travel options, still it would have taken him approximately two months to journey from Paris to his home in Bagnoregio.[15] The demands of administration must have weighed heavily on Bonaventure who, apparently, had delicate health from the time of childhood. Had he stayed on at the University of Paris, his life would have, undoubtedly, been different. He might have encountered Thomas Aquinas, his contemporary who taught at the Dominican School, and perhaps his theology would have ultimately influenced the Church in the same way as Thomas's did. Bonaventure's path, however, was to be distinct from the famous theologian-friar, for it was one marked by the challenges of an administrator's life and the constant need to clarify the meaning not only of being Christian but of being a follower of the little poor man, Francis of Assisi.

It is interesting that, prior to 1257, the year Bonaventure ascended to the office of Minister General, there is really no mention of Francis in either his life or writings. Of course this could easily be due to the fact that the details of Bonaventure's life are virtually unknown, and his writings are all scholarly ones produced at the University. After his election as Minister General, however, the figure of Francis becomes prominent in Bonaventure's thought. Bonaventure himself gives the first indication of this figure in the prologue to his classic *Soul's Journey into God* composed in 1259. He tells us that, following the example "of our most blessed father Francis," he went up to the mountain of La Verna seeking peace. It was on this mountain thirty-three years before, he writes, that Francis experienced the vision of a six-winged Seraph in the form of the Crucified. This vision is the basis of Francis's Stigmata.[16] Meditating on the experience of Francis, Bonaventure recounts, "I saw at once the meaning of this vision which represented our father's rapture in contemplation and the road by which this rapture is reached."[17] He then identifies the six wings of the Seraph as the six stages of the soul's journey that leads to the final stage of peace in God. Contemplating Francis's Stigmata in light of the soul's journey, Bonaventure had a sudden insight to the meaning of the Stigmata and exclaimed: "There is no other path but through the burning love of the Crucified."[18] Hans Urs von Balthasar captures this moment in Bonaventure's life when he writes:

> The Stigmata are the living, organizing center of Bonaventure's intellectual world, the thing that lifts it above the level of a mere interweaving of the threads of tradition. His world is Franciscan, and so is his theology, however many stones he may use to erect his spiritual cathedral over the mystery of humility and poverty. . . . And yet, when we have established that the Franciscan mystery is the center that crystallizes all, we have not yet uncovered the ethos that is peculiar to Bonaventure. For Bonaventure does not only take Francis as his center: he is his own sun and mission.[19]

It is not unreasonable to suspect that Bonaventure descended the mountain of La Verna transformed in the crucified Christ. He was, as Eric Doyle suggested, signed interiorly with the marks of the Crucified.[20] The marks of this transformation were revealed in Bonaventure's spiritual writings. He composed several works within a short period of time, all of which focus on the centrality of the crucified Christ as the center of true Christian life. These works included the *Soul's Journey into God, The Tree of Life, The Triple Way,* and *The Major Legend of Saint Francis.* Bonaventure, the theologian-turned-administrator, now revealed himself as a passionate lover of Christ. Affectivity marked his writings in a way that not even the Cistercians achieved (although he was influenced by them). Bonaventure's spiritual writings, which highlighted the humanity of Christ, contributed to a new medieval *zeitgeist,* a new current in spirituality in which personal relationship with Christ nurtured by use of the senses and imagination could lead one to union with God. Emphasizing devotion to the *humanity* of Christ, Bonaventure maintained that experience of God's love in Christ, especially in the crucified Christ, should lead to a truly loving relationship with God. As he wrote to a Poor Clare Nun: "Let your love lead your steps to Jesus wounded, to Jesus crowned with thorns . . . enter with your whole being through the door of his side into Jesus' heart itself."[21] Despite his solid theological training, Bonaventure held that lofty reasoning and persuasive argumentation were not the means to attain happiness and peace. Rather, poverty, prayer, the power of love, all rooted in the rich soil of the Scriptures, lead the faithful Christian to the overflowing goodness of God.

Although Bonaventure developed a spirituality grounded in the crucified Christ, following the exemplary life of Francis, he did not lose touch with the theological currents at the University of Paris. The bitter feud between the secular masters and mendicants continued and, in 1269, Bonaventure wrote *Defense of the Mendicants* to silence the complaints of the secular master, Gerard of Abbeville. Although this ongoing controversy was disturbing, it paled before the menace of a certain radical Aristotelianism that was making a definite inroad in the teaching of the faculty at the University of Paris. The primary source of this Aristotelianism was found in the writings of the Islamic philosopher, Averroes.[22] The adherents of this radical Aristotelianism taught positions in philosophy that seemed clearly incompatible with the Christian faith such as unity of the intellect, denial of personal immortality and eternity of the world.[23] Bonaventure did not oppose Aristotle *per se* since he drew upon the philosopher in his own writings; however, he vehemently opposed [Averroist] Aristotelianism as a self-sufficient philosophy in which conclusions could be accepted or rejected but not corrected by theology,[24] and his position was dramatic and forceful. Undoubtedly, he feared corruption of theology at the University of Paris where the friars continued to study. The main problem with Latin Aristotelianism that concerned Bonaventure resided in the relationship between theology and philosophy. For Bonaventure, theology was the "queen of sciences" since it led to true wisdom, while philosophy was the "handmaid of theology." In Bonaventure's view, philosophy was not meant to be an accumulation of knowledge supported by persuasive arguments; rather, it was to support theology which in turn was to lead one to holiness.[25] However, not all theologians agreed that philosophy had to be entirely subordinated to theology; some ideas could be argued philosophically independent of theology. Thomas Aquinas, for example, maintained that one could hold to the idea of an eternal world—at least philosophically. Bonaventure adamantly opposed the notion of an eternal world both on philosophical and theological grounds, maintaining that without a definite beginning and end, there is no real [exemplary] relationship of the created world to God.[26]

What was at stake for Bonaventure was nothing less than the roots of Christian belief, namely, the integral relation between God and creation centered in Christ. A misunderstanding of this relation could lead to heresy and paganism. While philosophy was concerned with ultimate reality in a way universally accessible to human reason, Bonaventure maintained that only the experience of Christ and knowledge of the Christian faith could provide understanding to ultimate reality that differed from that of philosophy. In light of the Christ mystery, Bonaventure held that all purely philosophical yearnings for truth must stand open to correction and possible completion in the light of the metaphysical implications of Christ. Ideas such as creation out of nothing *(creatio ex nihilo)*, finite creation, created matter (including the soul) and personal immortality all reflected a true Christian understanding of God rooted in Scripture. Anything not grounded in Scripture in Bonaventure's view was probably treading heretical waters.

With the friars studying theology at the University of Paris, it is not surprising that Bonaventure kept in close contact with the University, returning several times to deliver lectures to the students there. Striving to inculcate an authentic understanding of Christian life, he lectured on the ten commandments (1267), the gifts of the Holy Spirit (1268) and the six days of creation (1273). It is perhaps these last lectures, delivered one year before his death, that express the full-flowering of Bonaventure's thought. In the first of these lectures, Bonaventure put forth in a clear and concise manner the foundation of Christian knowledge, namely, Jesus Christ. Christ, he professed, is the center of all knowledge, for in Christ are hidden all the treasures of wisdom and knowledge.[27] Despite the majestic symbolism woven into these lectures that betray Bonaventure's own mystical spirit, there is, at the same time, the voice of the Minister General warning his listeners not to fall prey to false traps. Reading the opening sections of this first lecture, one gets the impression that some friars were being lured by ideas seasoned with heterodox Aristotelianism. Bonaventure begins this lecture by affirming that the faithful Christian committed to the Church should not "give away the holy to the dogs nor throw pearls before the swine" ("swine" being the Averroist Aristotelians).[28] Rationality and harmony, he claimed, show themselves in observance of the divine law, peace and the concelebration of divine praise but not in the spirit of carnality and cruelity; malice or the spirit of presumption. For these types of people, he exhorted, do not seek to praise and adore God but are filled with the splendors of knowledge [and pride]. "They build wasps' nests," he states, "without honeycombs, while the bees make the honey."[29]

Bonaventure admonishes and exhorts his audience with a sharp tongue and skillful rhetoric, although his emphasis on the centrality of Christ is unmistaken. He not only puts forth his doctrine on Christ as center in these lectures, but the first lecture in particular is like a blueprint for the entirety of his thought. Since everything comes from God and is destined to return to God, there is no other way of return than through Jesus Christ. Christ is center not only of the human person (the microcosm) but of the universe (macrocosm) as well. He is the center of all history and time. And not simply Christ, but Christ crucified, who in utter humility and self-emptying, reconciled that which was furthest away from God. This is the One who is absolute Center, the cosmic Christ, who in his crucified and glorified humanity mediates between God and humanity here and in eternal life.[30] Because of the centrality of Christ, Bonaventure maintains, knowledge must not be in vain nor be sought for the sake of pride. Rather, all knowledge must begin with Christ who is the basis of true metaphysics.

One wonders how Bonaventure would have concluded his lectures on the *Six Days of Creation* in which the final [set of] lectures were intended to focus on the life of eternal beatitude. But the lectures remain unfinished. It is possible that Bonaventure terminated the lectures in May of 1273 because of other duties, and had hoped to resume them later on. Historians indicate that he was made a Cardinal-Bishop of Albano by Gregory X in May 1273 and consecrated Bishop at Lyons in November 1273. (Rumor has it that he was washing dishes at one of the friaries outside Florence when the papal delegates arrived with the Cardinal's hat. Not wanting to stop his chore, Bonaventure asked that they hang the hat outside on a tree. Such, it is said, was the degree of his humility.) The reputation of Bonaventure as a theologian and able administrator must have been known at least within ecclesiastical circles, for he was asked by the Pope to participate in the Ecumenical Council at Lyons in 1274 in which church reform and reconciliation between the Greek and Latin churches was to take place. He resigned as Minister General in May 1274 and was succeeded by Jerome of Ascoli who later became Pope Nicholas IV.[31]

That Bonaventure participated in the Ecumenical Council at Lyons is fairly certain but beyond this event the details of his life are vague. He died in Lyons on July 15, 1274, two days before termination of the Council for reasons that are still obscure. Did he die of natural causes, such as heart failure, worn out by the demands of his position as Minister General? Or did other factors play a role in his untimely death? History will never reveal the secret for there seems to be no accurate historical account of Bonaventure's death. André Vauchez points out that the lack of details concerning Bonaventure's death is surprising since, in the Middle Ages, the least penitent or pilgrim who died in the odor of sanctity became the object of a cult and was provided with a biography after death, even though legendary and fictitious.[32] Indeed, it is rather surprising that a friar who occupied the highest office in the Order for almost two decades remains historically vague. What is more startling is that he was not raised up to the altar of canonization until nearly two hundred years after his death. The earliest account of Bonaventure's life dates from the time of his canonization in 1482.[33] Was the canonization process delayed by friars who felt that Bonaventure's administrative procedures compromised the primitive ideal of Francis? Or did his *Legend of Saint Francis* which became the official *vitae* of the Order, represent a politically-motivated attempt to forge the "real Francis" into a model of holiness for a clericalized Order serving the Church?[34]

Whatever delayed the recognition of Bonaventure's holiness, it seems to have faded with time. By the fifteenth century, Bonaventure's works became influential, particularly because the great theological syntheses were in crisis and mystical tendencies were on the rise. In a letter of 1426, for example, Jean Gerson was deeply shocked that the Franciscan Order had not shown more zeal in promoting the canonization of Bonaventure whom he considered the most reliable and commendable theologian. The Council of Florence in 1440 also reintroduced the works of Bonaventure in view of negotiations with the Byzantine Church.[35] Around 1450 the saint's remains were exhumed and an official identification of his body was made, at which time it was noticed that his tongue was still intact.[36] Although Bonaventure was buried in Lyons, his shrine was purportedly plundered by the Huguenots in 1562 and the urn containing his body burned in the public square. There is, of course, no real evidence. We do know, however, that the Pope who canonized him, Sixtus IV, a Franciscan and former General of the Order, declared Bonaventure a saint on 14 April 1482. Bonaventure was not only made "saint" but was declared a doctor of the Church by Pope Sixtus V on 14 March 1588.[37] He was given the title "Doctor Seraphicus" because of his emphasis on the passionate love of God.

Bonaventure's obscurity is perhaps fitting for one who desired nothing more than to be conformed to Christ crucified—poor, humble, and compassionate. Maybe what he discovered on that mountain of La Verna in 1259 was that love desires only the happiness of the beloved. To lose oneself in the mystery of the crucified Christ, where suffering yields to the wings of love, is to gain the happiness and peace of God. Perhaps for a moment, Bonaventure touched this happiness, and the fire deep within his soul was enkindled by the burning love of the Crucified. We will probably never know the details of his life, but then again, amidst the vagaries of history, the only real testimony is personal holiness.

Notes

1. The actual date of Bonaventure's arrival at the University of Paris, like many of details of his life, is ambiguous. Jacques Bougerol identifies the year as 1236, see *Introduction to the Works of Bonaventure,* trans. José de Vinck (Paterson, NJ: St. Anthony Guild Press, 1964), 5; Ewert Cousins states that Bonaventure went to Paris in 1234 or 1235, see *Bonaventure and the Coincidence of Opposites* (Chicago: Franciscan Herald Press, 1978), 32; Timothy Johnson locates the year around 1235 (see *Bonaventure: Mystic of God's Word* [Hyde Park, New York: New City Press, 1999], 11). Similarly, the date of Bonaventure's birth is also debated but most scholars identify the year as 1217. See, for example, Cousins, *Coincidence of Opposites*, 31; Bougerol, *Introduction*, 3.

2. Up until the twelfth century, theology was confined to monastic circles where the experience of God was described in various spiritual writings. The turning point came when Peter Abelard published his famous *Sic et Non* (Yes and No) in which he analyzed theological questions from the point of objective argumentation. Using this "scholastic" method of analysis, Peter Lombard composed the four books of the *Sentences* concerning God, Creation, Incarnation and Sacraments. The *Sentences* became the basis of all theological study in the Middle Ages.

3. Cousins, *Coincidence of Oppposites*, 34.

4. Bonaventure "Letter in Response to an Unknown Master" 13. Engl. trans. Dominic Monti, *Writings Concerning the Franciscan Order*, vol. 5, *Works of Saint Bonaventure*, ed. George Marcil (St. Bonaventure, NY: The Franciscan Institute, 1994), 54.

5. Cousins, *Coincidence of Opposites,* 34.

6. Alexander's remark was recounted in the bull of canonization of Sixtus IV. See Quarrachi edition n. 6 (I, xl).

7. Cousins, *Coincidence of Opposites*, 35.

8. See Monti, *Writings Concerning the Order*, 24.

9. Ibid.

10. David Saville Muzzey, *The Spiritual Franciscans* (Washington, DC: American Historical Association, 1914), 7–8. Muzzey describes the zealots as follows: "Until Bonaventure's time the strict minority [of zealots], although a part of protest, and subject to some persecution, were not schismatists. They had seen the order growing worldly and rich, building fine churches and competing for chairs of learning in the universities. They had seen it binding itself closer and closer in obligation to the pope, by the acceptance of various concessions and exemptions. They hoped for reform in this present age and for the continuance of the order, under the guidance of spiritually minded leaders, in the path of obedience to the Rule and Testament of Saint Francis." It should be noted that while many of the zealots adhered to the teachings of Joachim of Fiore not all of them were Joachites; however, the Joachites within the Franciscan Order were, indeed, zealous for their ideals.

11. Muzzey, *Spiritual Franciscans*, 8–9; E. Randolph Daniel, *The Franciscan Concept of Mission in the High Middle Ages* (St. Bonaventure, New York: The Franciscan Institute, 1992), 81–2. The election of John of Parma to the generalate was a sign of hope for the zealots who believed that John could help them realize their ideals. With the resignation of John of Parma, the zealots' hopes were shattered and they drew further apart from the lax majority. By the 1270's under the leadership of Peter-John Olivi in Provence and Ubertino da Casale, Liberato and Angelo Clareno in Italy, they became more solidified as a group known as the Spirituals and maintained strong ascetic-apocalyptic ideas. The Spiritual Franciscans underwent persistent persecution for dissemination of their ideas and were eventually condemned in 1334 by John XXII. On the persecution of Peter-John Olivi and the Spirituals see David Burr, *The Persecution of Peter Olivi* (Philadelphia: American Philosophical Society, 1976), 67–83.

12. Monti, for example, clearly rejects the notion that John was a Spiritual and offers several other reasons for John's resignation including opposition from friars of the more "liberal" persuasion. See *Works Concerning the Order*, 26–7.

13. Ibid., 27.

14. Muzzey, *Spiritual Franciscans*, 9. According to Muzzey, Bonaventure's generalate marks the dividing line between the two periods in the history of the Spiritual Franciscans: the first period extending from the early protests in the order to the deposition of John of Parma (the zealots); the second period extending from the Council of Lyons (1274) to the suppression of the Spirituals by John XXII in 1334.

15. Johnson, *Bonaventure: Mystic of God's Word*, 16.

16. It is worth noting here that the Stigmata are referred to in the plural since they signify the wounds of Francis. Francis received these mystical wounds on the mountain of La Verna in 1224 where, praying and fasting, he had a vision of a crucified man in the form of a seraph. The episode is recounted in the biographies of Francis by Thomas of Celano and Bonaventure.

17. Bonaventure, *Itinerarium Mentis in Deum* (hereafter *Itin.*) prol. 2 (V, 295). Engl. trans. Ewert Cousins, *Bonaventure: The Soul's Journey Into God, The Tree of Life, The Major Life of St. Francis* (New York: Paulist, 1982), 54 (hereafter *Bonaventure*).

18. *Itin.* prol. 3 (V, 295). Engl. trans. Cousins, *Bonaventure*, 54.

19. Hans Urs von Balthasar, *Studies in Theological Style: Clerical Styles*, vol. 2, *The Glory of the Lord: A Theological Aesthetics*, trans. Andrew Louth, Francis McDonagh and Brian McNeil (San Francisco: Ignatius, 1984), 263.

20. Eric Doyle, introduction to *The Disciple and the Master: St. Bonaventure's Sermons on St. Francis of Assisi* (Chicago: Franciscan Herald Press, 1983), 13.

21. Bonaventure, *De Perfectione vitae ad sorores* (hereafter *Perf. vit.*) 6.1 (VIII, 120). Engl. trans. José de Vinck , "On the Perfection of Life, Addressed to the Sisters," in *Mystical Opuscula*, vol. 1, *The Works of St. Bonaventure* (Paterson, NJ: St. Anthony Guild Press, 1960), 239.

22. For a discussion on Bonaventure and Aristotelianism, see Fernand van Steenberghen, *The Philosophical Movement in the Thirteenth Century* (London: Nelson, 1955), 56–74; R. J. Roch, "The Philosophy of St. Bonaventure—a controversy," *Franciscan Studies* 19 (1959): 221–26. Van Steenberghen points out that Bonaventure protested against the philosophy of Siger of Brabant in his sermons of 1267 and 1268 (p. 75). Bougerol also includes the writings of Siger of Brabant as part of Bonaventure's attack against Latin Aristotelianism. See *Introduction*, 26.

23. Bonaventure *Collationes de decem praeceptis* (hereafter *Decem praec.*) 2.25 (V, 514); *Hex.* 1.16 (V, 332).

24. Gilson *Philosophy of St. Bonaventure*, 4.

25. This is the principal thesis of Charles Carpenter's recent book *Theology as the Road to Holiness in Saint Bonaventure* (New York: Paulist Press, 1999).

26. For Bonaventure's position on the eternity of the world see II *Sent.* d. 1, p.1, a. 1, q. 2 (II, 19–23). For discussion of Bonaventure and Thomas on this point see Matthew D. Walz, "Theological and Philosophical Dependencies in St. Bonaventure's Argument Against an Eternal Word and a Brief Thomistic Reply," *American Catholic Philosophical Quarterly* 72.1 (1998): 75–98.

27. *Hex.* 1.11 (V, 331).

28. *Hex.* 1.1 (V, 329).

29. *Hex.* 1.2; 1.5–8 (V, 329–330). Engl. trans. José de Vinck, *Collations on the Six Days*, vol. 5, *The Works of St. Bonaventure* (Paterson, NJ: St. Anthony Guild Press, 1970), 1, 3–4.

30. *Hex.* 1.38 (V, 335).

31. Cousins, *Coincidence of Opposites*, 41.

32. André Vauchez, "Canonization of St. Thomas and St. Bonaventure: Why a Two-Century Gap Between Them?" trans. Edward Hagman, *Greyfriars Review* 12.2 (1998): 197.

33. Monti, *Works Concerning the Order*, 6.

34. Monti examines the obscurity surrounding Bonaventure's life in view of the "Franciscan Question," see Monti, *Works Concerning the Order,* 4; cf. Johnson who states, "The reasons why Bonaventure's holiness was not recognized immediately are complex but probably relate to his controversial position among the friars who saw his administrative attempts to mediate and unify the various factions of the Franciscan Order as a renunciation of the primitive ideal of Saint Francis," in *Bonaventure: Mystic of God's Word*, 18.

35. Vauchez, "Canonization," 207.

36. Ibid.

37. Ibid., 208–9; A. Abate, "Quando S. Bonaventura fu dichiarato "Dottore della Chiesa?" *Miscellanea Francescana* 37 (1937): 98–207.

Bonaventure's Thought

Trinity

A well-known Bonaventurian scholar once remarked that Bonaventure's thought is like a gothic cathedral. The two main towers of the cathedral, he claimed, are the Trinity and Christ[1] which join together the flying buttresses of humanity and creation. And should these two towers be taken apart, so too would humanity and creation collapse. For without the Trinity there is no Christ, and without Christ there is no Trinity. The Trinity and Christ hold together the grand cathedral of the universe.

Bonaventure's theology begins with the Trinity, and this means that his theology is rooted in a divine ground that is at once unity and diversity, a community of persons who are mutually intimate, having distinct personality and yet so ultimately compatible that they breathe forth life with the same breath. The word "Trinity" is mysterious and, to the human mind, incomprehensible. It means literally "tri–une," that is, three and one, and connotes the idea (and formula) that God is three divine persons—Father, Son and Spirit—in one divine nature. That Bonaventure never developed an independent treatment of the "one God" suggests that he did not view the Trinity as an intellectual datum but a doctrine with radical consequences for Christian life. The essence of Bonaventure's trinitarian thought, I believe, is best summarized by Catherine LaCugna in her introduction to *God For Us*:

> The life of God—precisely because God is triune—does not belong to God alone. God who dwells in inaccessible light and eternal glory comes to us in the face of Christ and the activity of the Holy Spirit. Because of God's outreach to the creature, God is said to be essentially relational, ecstatic, fecund, alive as

> passionate love. Divine life is therefore also *our* life. The heart of the Christian life is to be united with the God of Jesus Christ by means of communion with one another. The doctrine of the Trinity is, ultimately, therefore a teaching not about the abstract nature of God, nor about God in isolation from everything other than God, but a teaching about God's life with us and our life with each other.[2]

Bonaventure's writings on the Trinity indicate that he pondered this mystery throughout his life and came to understand in a profound way the integral relationship between the Trinity and creation centered in Jesus Christ. On one hand he saw the stamp of the Trinity on all levels of creation and, on the other hand, he saw this divine life impressed on the human soul. While in his earlier scholarly writings he examined the nature of the "inner" life of the Trinity, in his later spiritual writings he explored the mystery of the Trinity within the context of the Christian life. It is not unreasonable to say that, on the foundation of the Trinity, Bonaventure constructed his entire theological vision.

Although the Seraphic Doctor studied theology at a European university, he did not adhere to the trinitarian theology of Augustine which was influential in the west. Rather, he described a model of the Trinity that had its roots in the Greek patristic tradition, similar to the one described by the fourth-century Cappadocian fathers.[3] While Augustine's model of the Trinity emphasized the unity of God, one essence and three divine persons, the Cappadocian model highlighted the personal nature of God in the formula, three divine persons and one divine essence. Rather than placing emphasis on the unity of God's *substance,* the Cappadocians placed the emphasis on divine *persons.* The very term "person" undergirds relationship since to be a person is to be in relation to other persons. For the Cappadocians, each divine person is defined according to origin since what a [divine] person is in itself cannot be determined. A person, therefore, is a relation of origin. The eighth-century theologian, John Damascene expanded the idea of "person-in-relationship" by saying that the divine persons of the Trinity are not only related to one another but they mutually inhere in one another and draw life from one another. The term Damascene used to describe this mutual co-inherence was "perichoresis."[4] That is, the divine persons, intimately related to one another, are irresistibly drawn to each other, taking one's existence from the other, containing the other in him/herself, while at the same time pouring self out into the other. This notion of mutual co-inherence figures prominently in Bonaventure's thought, especially since his model of the Trinity, based on the good, is grounded in mutual relationships. Instead of using the Greek term *perichoresis*, however, Bonaventure used the Latin, *circumincessio*, meaning that the divine persons "move around one another" in a communion of love.[5]

While the Greek [Cappadocian] model of the Trinity was attractive to Bonaventure, other spiritual writers helped him to formulate his trinitarian theology more clearly. One writer in particular who had a profound influence on Bonaventure was the mysterious sixth-century writer, the Pseudo-Dionysius.[6] In his writings, the Pseudo-Dionysius claimed that God is self-diffusive goodness;[7] God is not simply Being but God is that Goodness which is beyond Being, and which gives rise to Being. While this concept is grist for the philosopher, Bonaventure was apparently impressed by the notion of ultimate divine goodness (which is really a platonic concept). In the New Testament, he writes, God reveals his name as Good (Lk 18:19 "No one is good but God alone"); whereas in the Old Testament, God revealed his name as Being (Exod 3:14 "I am who Am"). Since God reveals Godself as Good in the New Testament, the Trinity must be essentially grounded in the good. Francis of Assisi frequently referred to God as good in his writings (9 times), often proclaiming God's goodness in the superlative: "all good, supreme good, totally good, You Who *alone are good*."[8] Indeed, he placed such a profound emphasis on God as good that to ignore the goodness of

Francis's God would be to ignore Francis himself. It is possible, therefore, that Francis's understanding of God as good may have also influenced Bonaventure's thinking.

Although goodness became the essence of what God *is* for Bonaventure, goodness alone does not explain the Trinity of persons. In order to understand God as triune, Bonaventure turned to the writings of the Victorine scholar, Richard of St. Victor. The core of Richard's argument for a plurality of divine persons is not the Dionysian concept of the good *per se* but of charity.[9] Charity is the supreme content of the good, the highest form of the good. Thus, if God is good then God is also charity or love. Where there is fullness of divinity there is fullness of goodness, and where there is fullness of goodness there is fullness of charity. Richard's argument is concise and ingenius. Essentially, he indicates, if God is ultimately charity, charity cannot exist in God without some sort of plurality in Godself. We can pause to think about this in human terms. Can a person live in total isolation from others for an indefinite period of time, literally having no contact with other people, and grow in love? Probably not. Unless there is an "other" in that persons' life, love cannot grow apart from relationship. Similarly, God cannot be a single monad, a self-sufficient singular One. If this were true, God would not be love. Charity, as Richard showed, requires a plurality in God, and he locates this plurality on the level of person. If God were simply one person there would be no communication of goodness [love] to another. Thus, if God is to be perfectly lovable, there must be at least two persons in God.

While the notion of "two persons in love" makes sense to Richard, he concludes that if there are *only* two divine persons, there could only be love for one another. This would be neither the fullness nor the perfection of love, for the highest perfection of love demands that each of the two persons in love share that love with an "other." Thus, Richard indicates, there must be three divine persons: one who is totally gratuitous in love [the Father], one who is totally receptive in love [the Spirit], and one who is both gratuitous and receptive in love [the

Son].[10] Where there are three divine persons in mutual love, there is perfection.

Richard of St. Victor and the Pseudo-Dionysius enabled Bonaventure to clarify the meaning of God as ultimate goodness and love.[11] While these two concepts, essential to the divine nature, are integrally related, they are not entirely synonymous. To say that God is goodness is to say that God is self-communicative. To say that God is love is to say that God is personal. The Trinity, therefore, is both self-communicative goodness and personal love. For Bonaventure, these two essential characteristics of God's nature will play out in the origin of divine persons. As we will see, the Trinity of goodness reveals itself as a creative unity of persons "being-in-love."

To understand the unity of persons in Bonaventure's trinitarian theology is to locate their origin in the good. The very "source" of infinite goodness is the Father. Because the Father is unbegotten (that is, has no prior source), the Father is first or primal. As the infinite "first person," the Father is absolutely fecund and, thus, the fountain-fullness of goodness. It is difficult for the human mind to conceive of an infinite source of goodness but we can compare it to one of the natural wonders in North America, Niagara Falls. Anyone who has ever seen the torrents of gushing waters bursting forth over the falls has never failed to gasp in awe and wonder at the magnificent power of these waters. Imagine that the source of these bursting torrents of waters is infinite. Such an image, although a limited one, gives us an idea of what the Father's infinite goodness is like.

We may, at this point, indicate that Bonaventure's understanding of God the Father preempts any classical notion of patriarchy. The Father is not a self-contained Being who "rules over" another. Rather, the notion of the Father as origin of all reality by way of the self-diffusive good imparts another meaning to the Father that may be more aptly described as "servant." The "rule" of the Father is to give to another. Since the totality of self-gift characterizes the Father, the Father may be described as the true poor and humble servant, which is quite a different image from that of the controlling despot.[12]

For Bonaventure, the mystery of the Trinity is rooted in the mystery of the Father who is source and goal of all reality. He describes the mystery of the Father according to the structure of the coincidence of opposites, a structure of thought which characterizes other aspects of his theology as well. The first pair of opposites are unbegottenness and generativity. Because the Father is unbegotten, without source, the Father is generative, or source of others.[13] The Father is, indeed, "Father" because, in the diffusion of the good, he (infinitely) generates a Son. That is, the Father is constituted as Father in the fullest sense in the act of generation. The idea of generation could easily be misleading or, at least, misinterpreted. When we think of "generation" we think of "producing" or "giving birth to another." While these ideas are not entirely foreign to what Bonaventure is describing as the nature of the Father, they nevertheless connote "biological" generation. When Bonaventure describes the Father as generative, he is neither using the word "Father" nor "generation" in a biological manner. Because the mystery of God is described within the limits of human language, the natural tendency is to conceive of God as a human being: the Father then becomes like an elderly male figure. Such a misconception, however, thwarts the mystery of God and reduces God to a human projection.

When Bonaventure states that the Father is generative, what he is saying is that this infinite first principle of the Godhead, the Father, is infinitely rich in goodness. And since the nature of the good is to diffuse itself (that is, goodness cannot be self-contained and remain good), the Father is the fountain-fullness of goodness. The key to understanding the Father as source of goodness is in the term "self-diffusive." Concentrating on the meaning of "self-diffusive goodness" allows us, therefore, to grasp more deeply the mystery of the Father. To say that the Father is "self-diffusive goodness" is to say that the "self" of the Father is identified by the nature of the good to "diffuse" or communicate itself to another. Therefore, that which the Father *is*, is self-diffusive goodness—and nothing other!

Now since the Father is the first principle of the Godhead, whatever the Father does, is done absolutely. That is, the Father cannot give away "half" the good and keep the other half for him "self," especially since the "self" *is* diffusive goodness. Thus, whatever the Father gives is given totally and absolutely. If the Father is self-diffusive goodness, the Father totally and absolutely communicates that goodness to another. Here is the second pair of coincidence of opposites: the Father is fountain-fullness of goodness *and* totally self-communicative or self-emptying (*kenotic*) by nature of the good. The mystery of the Father, therefore, is fullness and emptiness; richness (in goodness) and poverty (by the nature of diffusion or *kenosis*). Because the Father is this mysterious coincidence of opposites, all opposites in reality are grounded in this mystery of emptiness and fullness. Of course, it is important to keep in mind that when we speak of the Father's poverty, it is held in union with the Father as fountain-fullness of goodness. Only because the Father is the infinite source of goodness can the Father be poor or self-giving as the infinite gift of goodness.

Returning to Richard's notion that the highest good is love, we can say that the self-diffusive goodness of the Father is not a general diffusion of goodness; rather, because it is the highest good, love, it diffuses personally to one other than the Father, and that is the Son. Bonaventure describes the Son as being generated by nature of the Father's goodness (*per modum naturae*). Since it is the nature of the Father's goodness to diffuse itself, the Son is the One who is generated by the Father's diffusive goodness. The Son, therefore, is everything the Father is in One other than the Father.[14] The relationship between the Father and Son, in Bonaventure's thought, is the very ground of all other relationships. An understanding of this relationship allows us to understand the deeper meaning of creation, and within creation, the centrality of Jesus Christ.

As the one who is generated by the Father's goodness, and is the object of the Father's love, the second divine person is truly and uniquely identified as Son. Bonaventure also uses the title "image" to describe this second person of the Trinity, since the Son is the true image or imitation of the Father. To say that the Son imitates the Father does not mean that, like the Father, the Son is unbegotten; however, it does mean that the Son, like the Father, is source of others. The Son, therefore, is the true and perfect expression of the Father.[15] As expression, the Son is the one, true image. Thus, if the Father is kenotic (or self-emptying), so too, is the Son; if the Father is poor, so too, is the Son. And since the Father, who is totally turned toward the Son (by nature of the good) is humble, so too, the Son's humility is expressed in being turned toward the Father. Both Father and Son, therefore, share a unique personal relationship of likeness and expression.

Although the titles, "Son" and "Image" appropriately describe the second person of the Trinity for Bonaventure, the title that he favored because it encompasses all relationships, is that of "Word."[16] The Son, as expression of the Father, is the Word of the Father. Bonaventure uses the analogy of language to help clarify the meaning of this title, "Word." He writes: "So that we may come to understand better the nature of this Word, we must distinguish between a mental word and a causal word. A mental word is thought itself, or the concept of our mind. But the word of which we are speaking here is the causal word."[17] The mental word here, the "thought," can be likened to the Father. When that thought expresses itself as causal word, we have the Word or the second person of the Trinity. Thus, the eternal "self-thinking" of the Father, that is, all the eternal ideas of the Father, are expressed in the Word. For this reason, Bonaventure refers to the Word as the "Art of the Father," meaning that the Word expresses the Father's ideas.[18] The Word is also the "exemplar" since, as the basis of all the divine ideas, the Word is the "archetype" or model of all that exists. The notion of exemplarity which is central to

Bonaventure's thought will figure more prominently in his understanding of creation and Incarnation.

The significance of the Word as expression of the Father (and, we might add, expression of the Father's self-diffusive goodness) is born out in the idea that, through the Word, the Father creates. This makes sense if we understand the Word as the Father's ideas *expressed.* Bonaventure writes that the title "Word" expresses not only a relation to the one speaking (the Father), but to that which is expressed (creation), to the sound with which it clothes itself (Incarnation), and to the knowledge effected in others through mediation of the Word (Scripture).[19] Thus, for Bonaventure, the title "Word" includes all relations: to the Father, and to creation, humanity, and Scripture. "A more fitting title," he states, "could not be found."[20] The Word is the One through whom all the Father's self-communications take place. The Word expresses the mystery of the Father precisely as goodness and love, as the fecund source of all that can be. In this one divine Word, according to Bonaventure, all possibilities and worlds exist.

Why is the Word so central to Bonaventure's thought? Precisely because it is center! The Word is *medium* or center between the Father and Spirit and shares "properties" of both. With the Father, the Word shares the "property" of being the source of others, since with the Father, the Word/Son "spirates" the Spirit. However, the Word also shares, with the Spirit, the "property" of receptivity since, like the Spirit, the Word is generated by the Father's self-diffusive goodness. It is in receptivity to the Father's goodness that the second divine person is Son or Word, generated by the Father's goodness, and expressing that goodness as Word.

Understanding the relationships of the divine persons, therefore, allows one to appreciate the centrality of the Word in Bonaventure's thought. The Word, as center, is the point of unity, harmony and order. In this way, the Word plays a significant role not only within the Trinity but in the relationship between God and creation. As the Word is the inner self-expression of God, the created order is the external expression of the inner Word. This is an important idea for Bonaventure and merits some attention. When we say that the Word is the inner self-expression of God, we immediately imagine a singular word. But the key is in the term "self-expression." If the Word is the self-expression of God [the Father], the Word is singular but the "content" of the Word is, in a sense, infinitely multiple because the "content" expressed in the Word is all the divine ideas. Everything that has existed since the beginning of time, everything that exists, and everything that will exist in the future, is grounded in the one Word of God. Thus, the created order is the external [or limited] expression of the inner Word. All of creation, with its manifold variations, expresses the one Word of God.[21]

Bonaventure claims that creation flows out of the deep intimate relationship between the Father and Son. Therefore, whatever created reality exists possesses in its inner constitution a relation to the uncreated Word. As the Word is the self-expression of the Father within the Godhead, the world is the external expression of that self-utterance which is not God. In this way, there is nothing in creation that exists apart from the Word; indeed, everything that exists has meaning precisely in relation to the Word. When the Word becomes incarnate, the eternal Word enters into union with creation through humanity, and the mystery of the Father is uttered in history and time.

While the relationship between the Father and Son is fundamental to Bonaventure's thought, such a relationship is completed in the divine person of the Holy Spirit. Returning to the notion of the Father as the source of goodness, Bonaventure states that there are two ways this goodness is communicated: one is by nature (the Son), and the other, by will (the Spirit). The Spirit, therefore, is generated by the will of the Father (*per modum voluntatis*).[22] What this means is that the Father is not only creative and personal in love (the Son), but the Father loves freely (the Spirit). Without divine freedom, expressed in the Spirit, God would be less than perfect love. He would be reduced to either a necessary Creator or an absolute dictator or both! Bonaventure, however, does not view God as divinely manipulative or controlling. Rather, he returns to the notion that God is love. The perfection of love requires three persons: the source of love (the Father), the emanation of love proceeding from pure liberality (the Son), and the sharing of that love which proceeds as an act of the will (the Spirit).

Bonaventure sees the relationship between the Father and Son in terms of such great intimacy that the Spirit proceeds from them as from one principle. That is, the Father and Son are one in fecundity of the divine will. We may compare these divine relationships of love to human relationships. When two people are in love, whether it be the love between a husband and wife or between two friends, they experience a bond of love between them. This bond of love is spiritual and is as real as the marriage or friendship itself. In marriage, the intimate relationship of love may be expressed in the conception of a child; however, in friendship the bond of love between friends may be of such reality or spiritual depth that when a friend dies there is not only loss of the person *per se* but of "something else," the spirit which formed the bond of friendship between them. We may say that the spirit proceeds from the mutual love between friends in a way similar to the divine Spirit which proceeds from the mutual love between the Father and Son. Bonaventure describes the Spirit, therefore, as the perfect act of divine will. As the fruit of mutual love, the Spirit is "gift."

The gift of the Spirit [in creation] is the gift of God's love and, indeed, that which unites us to the Father and Son.[23] The gift of the Spirit reveals to us God's freedom to love. Indeed, the fact that the Spirit is given to each of us personally means that God loves us freely and personally. God breathes through each of us through the gift of the Spirit, and loves each of us in a total and absolute way. Because of this love, we are caught up in the mystery of love between the Father and Son. Each one of us is a word in whom the Father's love is expressed. This is an incomprehensible mystery for us to grasp. It is only through the Word incarnate, Jesus Christ, that this mystery becomes intelligible and meaningful in terms of our relationship to God.

For now we can summarize Bonaventure's theology of the Trinity by saying that this *tri-une* community of persons-in-love is dynamic and expressive. It is a community of personal love marked by fecundity, overflowing goodness, and creativity. Because the Trinity manifests an eternal, dynamic creativity it is outward-moving. It cannot remain self-enclosed or self-sufficient. Bonaventure does not describe the Trinity as a cloistered community, as if everything else exists "outside God." Rather, Bonaventure's Trinity is a dynamic self-diffusion of goodness whose essential life is marked by personal gift. God is simply love. And since God is perfect love, God not only loves freely but desires to share that love with an other. It is the nature of God to give Godself away in love. God is, indeed, poor and humble. While creation is free (that is, an act of divine will), it bursts forth from the infinite dynamic self-diffusion of the love between the Father and Son. Bonaventure indicates that creation is a limited actualization of the infinite and dynamic life that marks the divine order. Just as communication of love to another within the Trinity marks divine perfection, so too, in creation, everything that exists is structured to be in a relationship of love. The community of triune love is the very basis of created life.

Reflections

1. Spend some time contemplating the Trinity as a communion of persons united in self-giving love. What does it mean to profess belief in the Trinity on a personal level? How does Bonaventure's theology of the Trinity highlight the meaning of "person" for you?

2. Reflect on Philippians 2:5–11 (the hymn of kenosis). Do you have the same attitude of Christ, that of being totally receptive and turned to the Father as self-communicative love? Do you share the Father's expression of love by allowing yourself to be turned toward

another? If not, what is preventing this attitude in you? Spend time reflecting on the Father as loving and humble. How should this change your actions/attitudes?

3. Spend time reflecting on the titles of the second divine person: Son, image, Word. Which one speaks to you? Why?

4. Who is the Holy Spirit for you? Does the Spirit draw you more deeply into the love between the Father and the Son? If so, how? If not, why not?

Notes

1. Ewert Cousins, "The Two Poles of Bonaventure's Thought," *Sancta Bonaventura 1274–1974*, 5 vols, ed. Jacques-Guy Bougerol (Grottaferatta: Collegii S. Bonaventurae, 1974), 4:153–76 (hereafter *S. Bonaventura* followed by volume and page number); Idem, *Coincidence of Opposites,* 49.

2. Catherine Mowry LaCugna, *God For Us: The Trinity and Christian Life* (New York: HarperCollins, 1991), 1.

3. For a discussion of Cappadocian trinitarian theology, see LaCugna, *God For Us*, 53–79. LaCugna follows this chapter with one on Augustine's trinitarian theology (81–109).

4. John Damascene, *Expositio fidei orthodoxae* 8.17 (*PG* 94.789); cf. Bougerol who claims that Bonaventure quotes Damascene in his writings over two hundred times in *Introduction*, 25.

5. I *Sent.* d. 19, p. 1, a.u., q. 4, concl. (I, 349); *Hex.* 21.19 (V, 434); *Itin.* 6.2 (V, 310). In his commentary on the *Sentences*, Bonaventure indicates that he appropriated the term *circumincessio* (in-cedere) from the Latin translation of John Damascene's *De fide orthodoxa* made in the twelfth century by Burgundio de Pise. See also LaCugna, *God For Us*, 272.

6. The Pseudo-Dionysius was a monastic writer who probably lived in Syria around the year 500 C.E. Some claim he was the Athenian convert of Paul described in the Acts of the Apostles (17:34) and known as Dionysius the Areopagite. Others maintain that he was either Bishop Denis of Paris or the monophysite Patriarch, Severus, who assumed the pseudonym "Dionysius." Despite many attempts at identifying this figure, the historical personage remains a mystery. His writings, however, have been more influential on the Latin West than any other Eastern mystic. For a summary of the Pseudo-Dionysius's writings and thought see Bernard McGinn, *The Foundations of Mysticism*, vol. 1, *The*

Presence of God: A History of Western Christian Mysticism (New York: Crossroad, 1991), 157–82; Andrew Louth, *The Origins of the Christian Mystical Tradition: From Plato to Denys* (New York: Oxford University Press, 1981), 159–78.

7. Pseudo-Dionysius, *De coelesti hierarchia* 4.2.1 (*PG* 3.177c); *De divinis nominibus* 4.1.20 (*PG* 588–592a).

8. Francis of Assisi, "Praises To Be Said at All the Hours." Engl. trans. Regis J. Armstrong, J.A. Wayne Hellmann, and William J. Short, *Francis of Assisi: Early Documents,* vol. 1, *The Saint* (Hyde Park, NY: New City Press, 1999), 162 (hereafter FA:ED I).

9. For the structure of Richard of St. Victor's argument of love, see his *De trinitate* 3.2 (*PL* 196, 926–27).

10. Richard of St. Victor, *De trinitate* 3. 14 (PL 196, 924–25, 27). Richard argues that there must be in God not only a *dilectum* but a *condilectum* as well; *condilectio* is found where a third is loved by two in harmony.

11. In his introduction to Bonaventure's *Disputed Questions on the Mystery of the Trinity*, Zachary Hayes describes the influence of Richard and the Pseudo-Dionysius on the structure of Bonaventure's trinitarian theology. See Zachary Hayes, introduction to *Disputed Questions on the Mystery of the Trinity*, vol. 3, *Works of Saint Bonaventure* (St. Bonaventure, NY: The Franciscan Institute, 1979), 3–40.

12. On patriarchy and *kenosis* of the Father, see Ilia Delio, "Bonaventure's Metaphysics of the Good," *Theological Studies* 60.2 (1999): 235–37.

13. I *Sent.* d. 27, p. 1, a. u., q. 2, concl. (I, 470b); Alejandro De Villalmonte, "El Padre Plenitud Tonal de la Deidad," *S. Bonaventura*, 4:221–42.

14. Zachary Hayes, "Incarnation and Creation in St. Bonaventure," in *Studies Honoring Ignatius Brady, Friar Minor,* ed. Romano Stephen Almagno and Conrad L. Harkins (St. Bonaventure, NY: The Franciscan Institute, 1976), 314; Ilia Delio, *Crucified Love: Bonaventure's Mysticism of the Crucified Christ* (Quincy, IL: Franciscan Press, 1998), 32.

15. *Hex.* 1.16 (V, 332). Bonaventure writes: "The Father begot his own likeness, that is, the Word coeternal with himself, and expressed a similitude of himself, and in so doing he expressed all that he could." Engl. trans. De Vinck, *Six Days of Creation,* 9; Zachary Hayes, "The Meaning of 'Convenientia' in the Metaphysics of St. Bonaventure," *Franciscan Studies* 34 (1974): 90.

16. Hayes provides a good discussion on the titles of the second person of the Trinity. See introduction to *Mystery of Trinity*, 48–53.

17. Bonaventure, "Sermon II on the Nativity of the Lord," in *What Manner of Man? Sermons on Christ by St. Bonaventure,*" trans. Zachary Hayes (Chicago: Franciscan Herald Press, 1989), 57.

18. *Hex.* 1.13, 16 (V, 331).

19. Bonaventure, *Commentarius in Evangelium Joannis* (hereafter *Comm. in Joann.*) c. I, p. 1, q. 1 (VI, 247); Hayes, introduction to *Mystery of Trinity*, 51.

20. Ibid. See also I *Sent.* d. 27, p. 2, a. u., a. 1 (I, 481ff).

21. See Hayes's discussion on the Word in his introduction to *Mystery of Trinity*, 51–2.

22. I *Sent.* d. 6, a.u., q. 2, resp. (I, 128).

23. I *Sent.* d. 18, a. un., q. 2 (I, 325–326); q. 4, resp. (I, 328); q. 5 (I, 329–331). The names which Bonaventure uses to designate the third person of the Trinity are love, bond, Holy Spirit, and gift. In the proper sense, the Holy Spirit is said to be gift since the title expresses both the Spirit's relation to the Father and the Son as well as to creatures.

Creation

In the first book of his commentary on the *Sentences,* Bonaventure writes that creation is like a river which flows from a spring, spreads throughout the land to purify and fructify it, and eventually flows back to its point of origin.[1] This image not only speaks to us of Bonaventure's appreciation for the beauty of creation but it also indicates that he saw the deep intimate relationship between creation and the triune God. It is an image that imparts to creation a vibrancy of life replete with the self-diffusive goodness of God. Creation flows from the divine fountain-fullness, the "spring" of the creative and dynamic Trinity.

Bonaventure describes creation as sharing in the mystery of generation of the Word from the Father; it is a limited expression of the infinite and dynamic love between the Father and Son, emerging out of this relationship and exploding into "a thousand of forms" in the universe.[2] He uses the term "emanation" (*emanatio*)[3] to describe the birth of creation from the womb of the triune God of love. Although the platonic use of this term means that creation necessarily flows out of the infinite, transcendent One, Bonaventure uses the term "emanation" in a Christian context. Creation, he writes, is like a beautiful song that flows in the most excellent of harmonies but it is a song that God *freely* desires to sing into the vast spaces of the universe.[4] That is, there is nothing that compels God to chant the hymn of the universe. Creation is simply the loving outflow of a loving God whose infinite dynamic goodness is shared in a limited dynamic way. Creation is God's "other." God doesn't *have* to create since God is infinitely fecund and self-communicative within Godself. God simply *desires* to create because God is love, and perfect love can never be self-contained but must be shared freely with another. The world exists, Bonaventure indicates, by virtue of the free creative power of divine love. Creation is a (free) act of divine goodness spilling forth from the infinite divine community of love.

To say that creation flows out of the infinite fountain of divine self-diffusive goodness is to say that God is creative and loving. The Word, as we have said, is the Art of the Father because the Word expresses all the divine ideas (of the Father). When that Word is uttered in time, the canvas of creation unfolds. The triune God is then revealed as a divine Artist, and creation is the finite expression of the Artist's infinite ideas. As a work of art, creation is intended to manifest the glory of the Artist-Creator. In order for divine glory to be consciously expressed, God creates human beings who are capable of participating and manifesting that glory.[5] As Zachary Hayes claims, a world that manifested the glory of God but did not include some creature able to perceive and revel in that glory would make little sense. In fact, such a world might suggest a selfish or a self-centered God.[6] But indeed, this is not the case. Rather, God freely creates a glorious universe and calls forth within this universe human persons who are endowed with the freedom to participate in this divine artistic splendor.

The beauty of creation on which Bonaventure reflected was evident in the order and harmony of the things of creation.[7] The beauty, order and harmony of creation signified to Bonaventure that this created world is not simply a stage for human activity or a backdrop to human longings, but that the whole of creation has meaning and purpose. It comes from God, reflects the glory of God, and is intended to return to God.[8] Creation, we might say, is like a cosmic symphony. Bonaventure's vision of creation, with its emphasis on harmony and order, was compatible with the Ptolemaic universe with which he was familiar. Such a closed universe was unlike the evolutionary one we know today but rather one characterized by harmonious order. The earth was at the center of the Ptolemaic universe and the seven planets circled perfectly around the earth, guided by the forces of the crystalline heavens. Unity and proportionality characterized this universe in the same way that creation itself was marked by unity in multiplicity. Within this Ptolemaic universe, Bonaventure saw that everything in creation is ordered one to another, since everything has its proper location, arrangement and purpose in this world. He saw things ordered not only *within* creation but he indicated that everything in creation is oriented and directed toward a *telos*, a final goal.[9] Bonaventure perceived such a harmonious connection between the historical and teleological orders that he described them joined in such a way that one is made to conform to the other.[10] That is, the ordering of things in the universe exists because of the ordering of things toward their final end.

With such an emphasis on the order and harmony of creation, it is no wonder that Bonaventure vehemently opposed the idea of an eternal world. Essentially, the notion of an eternal world means that the world has no beginning and no end. And if there is neither a beginning nor end, matter itself is eternal.[11] The eternity of the world, in Bonaventure's view, militated against the order of creation since, without a beginning and end, there could be no true order in creation. The world would be meaningless because it would have no real relationship with God and, therefore, no God-intended purpose or destiny. Without God as creator, matter itself would be eternal and, if matter is eternal, it can reflect nothing of God. Thus, Bonaventure concluded, the world is not eternal. Rather, it is created by God, in time, out of nothing, by one supreme principle whose power has disposed all things with a certain measure, number and weight.[12] Creation, therefore, has a definite beginning and a definite end. Only in this way does creation have meaning and purpose since only a finite creation can be ordered to an infinite God.

If one were to read Bonaventure's writings on creation and ask, what is the fundamental point of his doctrine, the answer would have to be relationship. Bonaventure's theology is relational primarily because the foundation of his theology, the

Trinity, is a community of relationships, and it is out of this community that creation emerges.[13] All of creation—rocks, trees, stars, plants, animals, and humans—are, in some way, related to the Trinity. Yet, we may ask, what do things such as rocks and plants share in common with God? With a keen sensitivity toward creation, Bonaventure must have entertained questions of this type because he devoted considerable thought to the material world, and by this, I mean the non-human created world of rocks, trees and stars. For one thing, he did not view the material world as "brute matter," that is, lifeless and inert. Rather, because the material world is created by God, it is like the Trinity itself, dynamic and relational.

Writing in support of the medieval doctrine of hylomorphism (a doctrine he acquired from Alexander of Hales), Bonaventure maintained that all finite beings are composed of matter and form, and are subject to change.[14] The language of matter and form is somewhat archaic to the modern mind but we can explain these notions by saying that form is what a thing is, that is, form is the concrete expression of a thing.[15] For example, a cross has the form of two bars at right angles to each other. The content of what the form expresses is matter. Thus, the two bars that form the cross may be composed of wood or iron or some other "matter" or material. When we speak of hylomorphism we mean that while matter remains the same, the expression of matter in the form of content may change. Hylomorphism underscores the fact that everything is subject to change and, if this is true, it means that everything exists in a state of potentiality. The material world, therefore, is not an accumulation of things fixed in time; rather, matter is simply the name that underscores the principle of potentiality. That is, matter is neither spiritual nor corporeal but can be informed by either spiritual or corporeal forms. Bonaventure not only held to a plurality of forms but he believed, like Augustine, that all forms, except the human soul, were co-created with matter at the beginning of the world and have since resided in matter, and will continue to do so until the end of time.[16] This doctrine of seminal principles imparts a very dynamic view to creation since it is "loaded" with a myriad number of possibilities or active potentialities inserted by God at the beginning of creation. When God creates, God does not bring about new essences but God brings to completion or actualization that which is incomplete or potential. In creation, therefore, what is implicit (potential) is made explicit (actualization of potential) by the power, wisdom and goodness of God.

By affirming the doctrine of seminal principles, Bonaventure indicates that matter is dynamic and filled with a multiplicity of possibilities (from the beginning of time until the end of time). Everything that will exist until the end of the world already exists potentially within matter. Although the actual insight as to how God creates is a mystery, Bonaventure maintains that God *freely* creates. Freedom is inherent in the order of creation. God grants freedom to creation without disrupting the divine intention to which creation is ordered. The fact that the human person emerges in creation, fit for receiving the divine into him/herself is, according to Bonaventure, the unfolding of the Divine Artist's plan. Bonaventure sees the human person as the crown of God's created order.[17] If matter is dynamic and oriented toward form, Bonaventure sees it oriented toward the highest form, the human spirit, open to union with God. He uses the term "spiritual matter" to describe the orientation of matter toward spirit.[18] In his commentary on the second book of *Sentences,* he states that God created matter lacking in final perfection of form so that by reason of its lack of form and imperfection, matter might cry out for perfection.[19] That is, God *could have* created the world as he intended it to be; however, he chose to create it in such a way that it would be gradually perfected. Herein, I believe, the notion of freedom plays an important role. For God could have established the world in perfection—in biblical terms—in an entire day rather than over the course of six days. But God's purpose in creating was not simply to establish an order of being. Rather God created in such a way that there would be one in creation (the human person) who would *freely* choose God, and in choosing God, become like God—perfect in love.[20]

Thus, God created in such a way so as to persuade humans to seek final perfection by teaching, moving and delighting them.[21] But is God concerned only for humans? Is creation simply to serve humanity? And, if so, is this not the type of anthropocentrism that offends the dignity of creation? Bonaventure states that the material world cries out for perfection but it is unable to attain this end on its own. Matter has a drive toward spirit but only one who is matter and spirit can unite the material world to God.[22] It is for this reason, Bonaventure states, that the human person stands at the center of creation—not to dominate it but to lead it to perfection. It is the human person, he writes, that uniquely reflects the Trinity in the threefold structure of matter, spirit, and the union of these.[23] The material world is dependent on the human person to attain its destiny in God. We might say that the spiritual destiny of the material world is bound up with the human journey to God. But in return it is the material world that helps the human person find God. In Bonaventure's view, neither humanity nor creation can exist apart from each other and attain true relationship with God. Only in mutual relationship is God's love fully expressed.

One of the most important metaphysical questions for Bonaventure concerned the likeness of relationships between God and the created world. The doctrine that defines these relationships is referred to as "exemplarism."[24] Exemplarism is based on the notion of the exemplar or model. Everything that exists, in Bonaventure's view, is a copy or replica based on a pattern or model. For the Ancient Greeks such as Plato and his followers, such models were not found in this world but were located in a world beyond, a transcendent world. Plato described this world as one of ideal forms. In this transcendent world of forms is found the true models of all things that exist. The only way to come to know the truth of things, therefore, is to transcend this world through contemplation.

Bonaventure's doctrine of exemplarism shares similarities with that of Plato. For example, he maintained, like Plato, that the model or archetype of everything that exists resides in a transcendent world. Unlike Plato's world of forms, however, which has nothing in common with the created world, Bonaventure located the world of forms (or archetypes) in the divine Mind, specifically, in the Word of God.[25] The divine Word, as we have said, is the dynamic expression of the Father's goodness. All of the divine ideas of the Father are expressed in the One (divine) Word. Of course, there is really only one idea, and this idea is the infinite content of God's self-knowledge. Thus, divinity not only knows itself and all that it can produce in the created world, but it knows all those things that it will produce, and those things which are mere possibilities and will never exist. It is for this reason that Bonaventure can say that all possible worlds exist in the Word.[26] In this one Word is everything that exists, that existed, that could ever possibly have existed or will exist in the future. Time is irrelevant to the eternal Word of God.

Because the Word of God is the center of the divine ideas, the Word is the model or exemplar of all things. All things are true in relation to the Word. Just as the eternal Word expresses the Father, so too, when the divine ideas of the Word are expressed, creation appears as the art of God. As the Word expresses the Father, creation expresses the Word.[27] This means that everything in creation has its model or exemplar in the Word of God. When the Word becomes flesh, the center of the Trinity in whom the truth of all reality exists, appears at the center of creation; thus, the truth of creation is revealed.

Bonaventure described the created universe as the fountain-fullness of God's expressed being. As God expresses himself in creation, creation, in turn, expresses the Creator. We can compare the manifold variety of things in creation to the stain-glassed windows of a great cathedral. Just as light strikes the various panes of glass and diffracts into an array of colors, so too the divine light emanates through the Word and diffracts in the universe, producing a myriad of "colors" expressed in a myriad of things, all reflecting the divine light in some way. Bonaventure used two images to describe creation: mirror and book. As a mirror, creation reflects the power, wisdom, and goodness of the Trinity precisely by the way things express themselves.[28] However, Bonaventure also describes the created world as a book in which its Maker, the Trinity, shines forth and is represented at three levels of expression: a trace (vestige), an image, and a similitude (likeness).[29] The difference in these levels of expression reflects the degree of similarity between the creature and Creator, the copy and the model.

The trace (or vestige) is the most distant reflection of God and is found in all creatures. That is, every grain of sand, every star, every earthworm, reflects the Trinity as its origin (efficient cause), its reason of existence (formal cause) and the end to which it is destined (final cause). Everything that exists, therefore, reflects the power, wisdom and goodness of the Trinity. The image, however, is only found in intellectual (human) beings. It reflects the fact that the human person is not only structured according to the image of the Trinity, but as image, the human person is an apt receptacle for the divine. The human person is structured to express the Trinity in a limited and finite way. Bonaventure describes those humans conformed to God by grace as similitudes, since, through grace, they bear a likeness to God.

Thus, for Bonaventure, creation is a theophany, an expression of God's glory manifested in the sacred order of creation. Because the world expresses the Word, every creature is itself a "little word"; the universe, therefore, appears as a book representing and describing its maker. Every creature is an aspect of God's self-expression in the world, and since every creature has its foundation in the Word, each is equally close to God (although the mode of relationship differs). Since the Word of God is expressed in the manifold variety of creation, Bonaventure views the world as sacramental; it is a symbolic world and one full of signs of God's presence. The world is created as a means of God's self-revelation so that, like a mirror or footprint, it might lead humans to love and praise the Creator. It is a meaningful world, a world "pregnant with God," as Angela of Foligno once exclaimed.[30] The world is a sign and is meant to lead humans to what it signifies, namely, the infinite Trinity of dynamic, eternal and self-diffusive love.

The book of creation, according to Bonaventure, was intended by God to be the book of divine wisdom made visible to all. As we will see later on, the book of creation became unintelligible to humans because of sin.[31] Like a book written in a foreign language, Bonaventure states, creation became illegible because the human mind, clouded by sin, became enveloped in darkness. When sin rendered this book incomprehensible, Wisdom herself, the Word, became flesh, so that the book written within (the divine Word) became written without, in the humanity of Jesus Christ. In the Incarnation, the ground of all reality, the divine Word, appeared at the center of creation. The Word who is the truth of all things took flesh and was made known in the person of Jesus Christ. One who knows Christ, therefore, knows the truth. Bonaventure saw the connection between the exemplary world and the centrality of Christ in the life of Francis of Assisi. In his biography of Francis, he describes the exemplary world—as it was intended to be. For Francis, who was conformed to Christ saw the truth of each and every thing in its relation to God. As Bonaventure writes:

> In beautiful things he contuited Beauty itself
> and through the footprints impressed in things
> he followed his Beloved everywhere,
> out of them all making for himself *a ladder*
> through which he could climb up to lay hold of him
> *who is utterly desirable.*
> With an intensity of unheard devotion
> he savored
> in each and every creature
> —as in so many rivulets—
> that fontal Goodness.[32]

Bonaventure highlights Francis as the exemplary Christ-mystic. Francis is one who saw divine Beauty in the beautiful things of creation because he saw that beauty first in Christ as he was crucified and glorified upon the cross. Through his relationship with Christ, he identified each and every creature as a brother and sister because he recognized that they had the same primordial source [or goodness] as himself. Bonaventure describes this ability to see the truth of things in relation to God as contuition. Contuition is the consciousness of God's presence together with the object of creation itself whether it be a tree, a flower or a tiny earthworm.[33] Francis was able to apprehend the real depths of creation because he had entered deeply into the Word incarnate. There, in the center of his being, and now, at the center of creation, he discovered the truth of himself and of all creation in God. Through his relationship with Christ, Francis, we might say, experienced a transformation of consciousness through grace. His awareness of the created world changed. The created world was no longer an illegible book to him; rather, every aspect of creation spoke to Francis of the love of God revealed in Jesus Christ. Francis was able to read the "words of creation" as the book of God. Earthworms, twigs and branches, poor beggars and lepers, all spoke to him of the love of God manifested in Christ. And he made of all things a ladder to climb up and embrace *Him who is utterly desirable.*

Through the life of Francis we can appreciate the mystery of Jesus Christ as the mystery of the Word by which we come to know the truth of all reality. Christ belongs to the very structure of reality: as Word, to the reality of God; as incarnate Word, to the reality of the universe created by God. It is Christ who reveals to the world its own meaning.[34] Since creation is a vast symbol in which God speaks his own mystery into that which is not himself, creation bears a "congruous" relation to the Word. Because creation is the "expressed word" of the divine Word, it is directed in its inner core to fulfillment and completion in God. But how shall it attain its goal? For Bonaventure, the goal is attained through the human person who, like Francis, is conformed to God through grace. The way to God is through Jesus Christ. Such a person recognizes the divine signs of creation and offers to God praise and thanksgiving. The human person who can offer a conscious loving voice to an otherwise mute creation[35] fills the yearnings of the divine heart: the praise and glory of God chanted by the human person who leads creation in a harmony of love. God desires that all of creation, with humanity at its center, live in peace and reconciliation. The reality of peace, however, is the order of love. Only the human person has the freedom to choose this reality because only the human person has the capacity to love in union with God. The destiny of creation, therefore, depends on how we love.

Reflections

1. Spend time in prayer or writing in your journal using these images: womb of God, fountain-fullness, divine artist, singer of the universe, God the creator.

2. Spend time outdoors trying to read the book of creation. Does creation impel you to seek God more deeply? Are you conscious of creation as a reflection of God?

3. Pray using Colossians 1:15–20. What does this demand of your relation to creation? Are you conscious of your relatedness to creation or do you see yourself superior to it?

4. Human persons are structured in a particular way to receive the divine. What is hindering you from fulfilling your vocation as a human person?

Notes

1. I *Sent.* prooem. (I, 1–6).

2 . Alexander Gerken, *La théologie du verbe: La relation entre l'Incarnation et la Création selon S. Bonaventure*, trans. Jacqueline Greal (Paris: Éditions Franciscaines, 1970), 132; Hayes, "Incarnation and Creation in St. Bonaventure," 314.

3. *Hex.* 12.3 (V, 385).

4. See I *Sent.* d. 44, q. 1, a. 3, concl. (I, 786a). "Optime ordinatae sunt rest in finem, salvo ordine universi, quia universum est tamquam pulcherrimum carmen, quod decurrit secundum optimas consonantias."

5. II *Sent.* d. 1, p. 2., a. 2., q. 1., concl. (II, 44b). Bonaventure frequently cited Proverbs 16:4.

6. Zachary Hayes, "Bonaventure: Mystery of the Triune God," in *The History of Franciscan Theology*, ed. Kenan Osborne (St. Bonaventure, NY: The Franciscan Institute, 1994), 64.

7. See *Itin.* 1.14–15 (V, 299).

8. Bonaventure, *Commentarius in librum Ecclesiastes* 1.7 (V, 13b); *Brev.* 2.11.2. Engl. trans. José de Vinck, *Breviloquium*, vol. 2, *Works of Bonaventure* (Paterson, NJ: St. Anthony Guild Press, 1963), 101.

9. I *Sent.* d. 47, a. u. 3, concl. (I, 844a-b). Bonaventure writes: "Duplex enim est ordo rerum: unus in universo, alter in finem."

10. II *Sent.* d. 15, a. 2, q. 3 (II, 387); *Hex.* 3.6 (V, 344).

11. Efrem Bettoni, *Saint Bonaventure*, trans. Angelus Gambatese (Notre Dame: University of Notre Dame Press, 1964), 57–9.

12. *Brev.* 2.1 (V, 219).

13. Alexander Schaeffer, "The Position and Function of Man in the Created World According to Bonaventure," *Franciscan Studies* 20 (1960): 266–67; Leonard Bowman, "The Cosmic Exemplarism of Bonaventure," *Journal of Religion* 55 (1975): 183.

14. Hayes, "Bonaventure: Mystery of Triune God," 69–70; Bettoni, *Bonaventure*, 73.

15. In his book *Passage to Modernity*, Louis Dupré discusses the Greek understanding of form, indicating that form comprises both the essence of the real and our knowledge of it. That is, it belongs to the essence of the real to appear, rather than to hide, and to appear in an orderly way. While Plato raised the form principle to an intellectual level inaccessible to sense preception, form continues to appear, though not immediately in sense perception but in an intellectual intuition. See Louis Dupré, *Passage to Modernity: An Essay in the Hermeneutics of Nature and Culture* (New Haven: Yale University Press, 1993), 18–19.

16. Hayes, "Bonaventure: Mystery of Triune God," 72–9. For a discussion on Bonaventure's view of matter and form, see Kent Emery,

"Reading the World Rightly and Squarely: Bonaventure's Doctrine of the Cardinal Virtues," *Traditio* 39 (1983): 188–99.

17. *Brev*. 2.4 (V, 222).

18. II *Sent.* d. 17, a. 1, q. 2, resp. (II, 414–415).

19. II *Sent.* d. 12, a. 1, q. 3 concl. (II, 298); Emery, "Reading the World Rightly," 195. Bonaventure further indicates that God chose to effect this gradual perfection [of matter] over a course of six days because six, the sum and multiple of its integers, is the perfect number."

20. As Hayes states, "man is creation that has become aware of itself in knowledge and freedom." See Hayes, "Incarnation and Creation," 318.

21. II *Sent.* d. 15, a. 2, q. 1, concl. (II, 383).

22. Bonaventure, *De reductione artium ad theologiam* (hereafter *Red. art.*) 20 (V, 324).

23. Schaeffer, "Position and Function of Man," 295.

24 . Exemplarism is defined as the doctrine of the relations of expression between God and creatures. See J. M. Bissen, *L'Éxemplarisme Divin selon saint Bonaventure* (Paris: J. Vrin, 1929), 4; Bowman, "Cosmic Exemplarism," 183–98.

25. I *Sent.* d. 35, a. u., q. 2 (I, 605); *Hex.* 1.13 (V, 331); *Hex.* 3.4 (V, 343).

26. III *Sent.* d. 1, a. 2, q. 2, ad 2 (III, 26). The possibility of many world orders is related to the fruitfulness of God's goodness which ultimately must be traced back to the fecundity of the Father who communicates goodness to the Word. Thus, the possibility of many world orders is expressed in the Word.

27. Bowman, "Cosmic Exemplarism," 185; Hayes, "Incarnation and Creation," 314.

28. *Itin*. 2.1 (V, 300).

29. *Brev*. 2.12 (V, 230).

30. *Angela of Foligno: Complete Works*, trans. Paul Lachance (New York: Paulist Press, 1993), 170. Angela of Foligno was a lay Franciscan penitent and a profound mystic whose devotion to the humanity of Christ led her to the highest stage of union with God. She died in 1309.

31. *Hex.* 2.20 (V, 340).

32. Bonaventure, *Legenda maior* (*Leg. maj.*) 9.1 (EM, 74). The critical edition of Bonaventure's *Legenda maior* used here is the *Legenda maior S. Francisci Assisiensis*, ed. PP. Collegii a Sancti Bonaventurae (editio minor) (Quaracchi: Collegii Sancti Bonaventurae, 1941), 2–125. References to the Latin text are listed in parentheses as EM and page number. Engl. trans. "The Major Legend of Saint Francis" in *Francis of Assisi: Early Documents*, Vol. II, *The Founder*, 596 (hereafter FA:ED II).

33. Bowman, "Cosmic Exemplarism," 197.

34. On the integral relation between Christ and the cosmos see Zachary Hayes, "Christology-Cosmology," *Spirit and Life: A Journal of Contemporary Franciscanism* 7 (1997): 41–58.

35. Hayes, "Bonaventure: Mystery of Triune God," 68.

Humanity

Bonaventure was a mystic of harmony and unity. In a world in which everything had its place, decreed by divine order, it was reasonable for him to envision a harmonious universe; for such harmony was ordained by a perfectly loving God. "For the perfection of the universe," he writes, "there had to be a creature endowed with a two-fold sense to understand the book written within [the soul] and without [the visible world], that is wisdom and its works."[1] This creature is the human person who sees the world as a "very beautiful song that flows along in the most excellent harmonies."[2] What is the "harmony of the universe" that Bonaventure described? How did he envision a "perfect universe"? Bonaventure saw perfection as the capacity to manifest and represent God in God's power, wisdom and goodness.[3] Translated into terms of human action, I believe Bonaventure's understanding of perfection could be described in terms of relationship: the power to reconcile, the wisdom to see, and the capacity to love. As we indicated in the last chapter, Francis, the man of peace, lived perfectly reconciled to the world around him. Through his deep relationship with Christ, he developed a piety that drew him up to God, attracted him to his neighbor, and—symbolically—returned him to the state of original innocence through universal reconciliation with each and every thing.[4] Through the lens of Francis's life, Bonaventure indicated that humanity is responsible for the perfection of creation, and by this he meant that creation is to attain unity with God.

Unlike some evolutionists today who suggest that humanity is simply a dot along the evolutionary scale, eventually to be replaced by another (more advanced?) species, Bonventure saw humanity as the crown and center of creation.[5] Writing within the biblical creation account of six days, Bonaventure states that humanity was created on the sixth or last day of creation as the greatest of God's works. The whole creation process leads up to and culminates in the creation of human persons. Although Bonaventure placed the human person at the center of creation, he did not view this position as one of domination or power. Rather, he viewed it as a position of *mediation.*[6] Because God created two extreme forms of finite beings—material beings and spiritual beings—he created between these two extremes a finite being (the human person) in whom the extremes are reconciled in a harmonious way. The human person, therefore, occupies a central position in creation not to dominate but for the purpose of harmony and peace.

The basis of humanity's centrality lies in the fact that the human person is a unique creation marked by a body-soul relationship. Although Bonaventure described the properties of the human body and soul respectively, he did not view these as separate entities but as uniquely one. The true nature of the human person, he claimed, is not an isolated spirit but a body-soul relationship, the perfect union of which reflects the power, wisdom and goodness of God. While the question today on the nature of the soul is drawing much attention in light of the new science, for Bonaventure such a question was meaningful in light of classical ideas. The soul, he claimed, has its own form and is brought into being by God out of nothingness (*ex nihilo*). The soul has life—essential life. It has intelligence and freedom, and is capable of beatitude.[7] The soul is willful, self-determining and free from all compulsion, that is, the soul cannot be forced to act; it is truly free. And because of this, the soul is destined for immortal life. Bonaventure describes the soul as having various powers: vegetative power by which the soul can be nourished and grow; sensitive power, by which the soul can apprehend sensible objects through its spiritual senses (touch, taste, smell, sight, and hearing); and finally, the soul has intellectual power. It can discern truth, reject evil and desire good.[8] The soul, therefore, is the center of all human activity. But it is not self-sufficient. Even though the soul is entirely spiritual, created (immediately) by God, it is dependent on the body which is formed out of the dust of the earth, created subject to the soul, and proportioned to it.[9]

One may suspect that Bonaventure's understanding of soul and body smacks of dualism, as if two separate entities—soul and body—were joined together by the Master-Artist (God) to form the human person. This, however, is not the case, for Bonaventure maintains that matter is inclined toward spirit. Had he encountered the writings of Pierre Teilhard de Chardin in the twentieth century, he might have affirmed Teilhard's notion that matter and spirit form a continuum, that is, matter tends toward spirit. Even in his own writings, however, Bonaventure affirmed a harmonious relationship between soul and body that preempts any type of dualism. He writes that when God created the body, he joined it to the soul, uniting these two in a natural and mutual relationship. God assigned the governance of the body to the soul so that the soul should be ordained to the body and govern it for the sake of acquiring merit.[10] The human body, on the other hand, possesses the noblest constitution and organization that exists in nature, possessing the "greatest variety of organs endowed with the greatest beauty and skill and manageableness."[11] The human body, therefore, possesses beauty. As in creation itself, the human body, with its many parts, manifests a certain order and harmony; yet what maintains this order of the body is the soul which governs it. Thus, Bonaventure views the soul as the highest part of the human person since God rules the soul directly by illumination while he rules the body by free will. In this way, the body and all its functions are subject to the spirit, while the spirit is subject to God.[12]

The relationship that Bonaventure describes between body and soul recapitulates his understanding of the material world with its spiritual potency. The human person, he writes, is a microcosm of the macrocosm (or universe).[13] For the human person, as for the universe itself, perfection only comes about through true union of matter and spirit. In Bonaventure's terms, the material world is incapable of any personal relation with God. It is, however, involved in this destiny in and through the destiny of the spiritual creation.[14] As a whole, the material world is ordered toward the human person who stands in the center of creation as the most noble of forms, uniting in a single entity matter (body) and spirit (soul). Because the soul is united to the body, it is united to the corporeal or material world. Thus, there is no spiritual fulfillment apart from material reality, either temporally or eternally. Even in eternal life, Bonaventure claims, the soul cannot be fully happy unless the body is returned to it, for the two have a natural ordination to each other: "Just as the soul, by reason of the body and to gain merit now lives on earth, so will the body, by reason of the soul and to gain reward some day live in heaven."[15] From this we may gather that material and spiritual natures are ordained to one another and will not rest until they are harmoniously united.

The human person is a subject of mystery, and Bonaventure identified this mystery precisely in the depths of the human person who is created in the image of God. "Image," as we said before, means imitation—expressed likeness. The human person, therefore, is created as the "expressed likeness" of God. We know God precisely in and through human nature. The notion of image is biblical. In the book of Genesis we read that we are made in God's image and likeness (Gn 1:26). Yet, in the oldest creation account of Genesis we read that we are given life by the breath of God, and with God's breath comes the gift of freedom to choose good and evil (Gn 2:7, 17). The human person is not only an image of God, therefore, but an image grounded in freedom. Although Bonaventure does not expound on the explicit connection between the divine image and freedom, such a relationship is essential to his thought and, we might say, the whole of his theological vision.

In his early scholarly writings, Bonaventure described the human person as created in the image of God, meaning that God is actually in the soul as an object naturally known and loved.[16] Humans are structured in a way that they are able to receive God into their being; humans are able to know God, and in knowing God, to love God in a way that imitates God's own love for creation. The three faculties that comprise the divine image are memory, intellect and will.[17] Drawing upon the writings of Saint Augustine, Bonaventure indicated that humans have something of God already within their memory (what more contemporary writers would call a "prethematic" grasp of God). Memory is that vast field, as Augustine described it, wherein is the past, present, and future. It is deep within the labyrinth of the human mind where essential principles of human thought shape conscious knowledge. When that implicit presence of God stored in the memory becomes conscious, it awakens one to the knowledge of God; and once the knowledge of God is experienced, it yields to the love of God. Through the powers of memory, intellect, and will, therefore, human beings are formed to the likeness of the Trinity and, by virtue of these powers, they are able to discover truth and embrace goodness. The human person has the capacity for God because the human person can know and love God and, thus, is able to partake of God's life.[18]

Although Bonaventure was deeply impressed by Augustine's doctrine of the divine image, he was also aware that the capacity of the human person for God is not simply a psychological function. That is, the image of the human person is not something contained *within* the mind. "Image" is not a "part" of human nature. Rather, image is what the human person is in relation to God. It connotes expression, imitation and, as such, is dependent on relationship. The relationship, of course, that translates image into expressed likeness is relationship with God. But even this does not get to the heart of the matter for Bonaventure, for this relationship means really coming to the truth of oneself which can only be found in God. Image, therefore, is intimately related to identity—the truth of who we are or, rather, who we are created to be—and this can only be found in God. For Bonaventure, the search for identity is not one that takes place in the world; rather, it takes place within the soul, since God is more intimate to one's self than one is consciously aware. This intimate nearness of God is the image in which each of us is created; thus, to enter into this image is to enter into the truth of one's identity. To discover the truth of one's identity is to discover God because the secret of one's identity is hidden in the love and mercy of God. Bonaventure writes: "I will see myself better in God than in my myself."[19] To "see" oneself in God is to know God since whatever is in God is really identical with him. Thus, the only way one can be oneself is to become identified with him in whom is hidden the reason and fulfillment of one's existence. One who finds God finds oneself and to find one's true self is to find God.[20] This is the basis of peace and happiness that Bonaventure will later explore in his *Soul's Journey Into God.*

While the truth of one's being is found in God, it is God alone who can teach one to find God. Bonaventure explores this idea through the integral relationship between the human person and the Word of God. He writes that the human person is in the image of God not in a general sense of being like God but in a specific sense of being like the Son.[21] The capacity of the human person to be an image of God, therefore, is grounded in the Word as image of the Father. Just as the Word is the expressed "image" of the Father, the human person is created to be an expressed "image" of the Word. We might say that God utters each of us like a word containing a partial thought of himself. And when that word is spoken in and through our lives, God is made visible in the world.

Bonaventure used the term *convenientia ordinis* to describe the inner ordering of the human person to the Word.[22] This means that there is a congruent relationship between the human person and the Word of God so that a person is truly an image in relation to the Word. When the Word becomes flesh in the Incarnation, the truly human image of the divine is expressed in the person of Jesus Christ. As image of God, therefore, Christ not only reveals God to us but he reveals who we are in relation to God, that is, the truth of our humanity. This becomes important to Bonaventure because he sees the poverty and humility of Christ not only expressive of God as love but expressive of the human person who, being created by

God, is by nature poor and humble. The truth of one's self in God, therefore, is found in relationship to Jesus Christ. The more we enter into the mystery of Christ, the more we discover God and our selves in God. To be an image of God, in Bonaventure's view, is to be a truly human person—not an individual enclosed in self—but one in whom God's life shines through.

Because Bonaventure maintains that God is essentially love, he sees the life of God (who is love) most clearly expressed in the crucified Christ. The person who freely enters into the truth of one's self in God, therefore, enters into the mystery of the cross, for here in the image and likeness of the crucified Christ is the reflection of who we truly are in our humanity and what we are created to be in relation to God, that is, vessels of compassionate love.[23] It is God's love that transforms us into the truth of our created being, and when we arrive at that truthfulness of our being and are restored in love, we become the image and likeness of Christ. Christ shines through us in our flesh, and this is none other than the radiance of God's love. Through the grace of the Holy Spirit, therefore, we become, like Christ, an expressed word of God's self-communicative love. This is why the Stigmata of Francis signify to Bonaventure Francis's utter Christ-likeness because they represent the true image of Francis, perfectly restored by the grace of God and transformed by divine love. In his *Major Legend of Saint Francis* he writes:

> After true love of Christ
> *transformed* the lover *into His image,*
> . . . *the angelic man* Francis
> *came down from the mountain,*
> bearing with him
> the likeness of the Crucified,
> depicted not on *tablets of stone* or on panels of wood
> carved by hand,
> but engraved on parts of his flesh
> *by the finger of the living God.*[24]

It is Christ, therefore, who fills the created image with the eternal exemplary Image so that humanity may reach its fullest potential in God.[25] To be perfectly conformed to the likeness of God is to become a similitude; it is to be like Christ, willing to suffer and die for the sake of one's neighbor and for the love of God. The human image of God is expressed in love.

What makes Bonaventure's theology of image so distinct is that it reflects the very structure of human persons to imitate. Humans are mimetic by nature.[26] From the very moment of birth, humans learn how to act by imitating others: babies imitate children; children imitate parents; and parents imitate heroes. In a sense, what we become is shaped by who we imitate. When imitation leads to rivalry, sin results. Without stating it in precisely these terms, this is how Bonaventure describes original sin. Desiring to be like the Son, he states, who alone is the perfect Image of the Father, humanity fell into sin. Bonaventure describes a time before sin, a time of original justice and peace when humans created with sanctifying grace stood upright before God.[27] Because human nature was endowed with grace, humans were originally turned to God by nature. In this standing upright in grace before God, humans imaged God—their understanding was in accord with the highest truth in the act of knowing; their will was conformed to the highest good in loving; their strength was joined with the highest power in doing good. Bonaventure writes: "For humanity is upright when the intelligence coincides with the supreme truth in knowing, the will is conformed to the highest good in loving, and strength is united to the supreme power in operating."[28] It is hard to imagine that such a time once existed for humanity; yet, Bonaventure maintains there was a time when humans, rapt in perfect contemplation, shared in the ultimate goodness of God. According to Bonaventure, humans saw the truth of all reality in the embrace of God's love. As he writes:

> The whole person, created by God, was placed in paradise and given a two-fold perception, interior and exte-

> rior, consisting of the mind and flesh, and a double range of senses, inner and outer, one in reason and one in the flesh. . . . Through the eye of flesh, the human could see things outside in creation, with the eye of reason, the things within, with the eye of contemplation, the things above.[29]

In the beginning, therefore, the human person stood freely before God, as an image of God, at the center of creation, glorifying God in and through the things of creation.

This idyllic vision of creation with humanity at the center compels Bonaventure to identify the basis of a fragmented world in the free will of the human person. In the prologue to the commentary on the second book of the *Sentences* he writes: "God made the human person upright, and s/he has entangled him/herself in an infinity of questions."[30] Bonaventure does not offer a detailed explanation on how humanity lost the peace of paradise and fell into a state of sin. But the very fact that the human person became "entangled" in "infinite questions" gives us a clue. The ability of humans to question leads us to suspect that humans exerted a stronger intellectual power than they originally had. It seems that what Bonaventure is describing here corresponds to Karl Jasper's notion of an axial period of consciousness. Whereas in the pre-axial period, a time characterized as tribal, mythic and cosmic, humanity lived in close harmony to the earth; in the axial period, humans developed a sense of autonomy, of individuality, and with this sense, an awareness of a self-transcendent nature. Humans became aware of an ultimate transcendent ground of Being. With this awareness, however, also came the experience of freedom, that is, individual freedom to choose for one's self.[31] Sin, we might say, is freedom gone awry. For instead of choosing God (and thus, acting in perfect love), humans chose the "self" in order to be equal to God. Bonaventure describes the fall due to sin as a turning away from the good and a turning toward creatures, investing in others the goodness and truth that rightly belongs to God.

Turned away, entangled in questions, the human person became enveloped in darkness, wandering in the world, seeking the good that was lost. Although humans lost the ability to stand upright before God, becoming bent over due to sin, Bonaventure claims they lost the habit of this ability, not the ability itself. With sin, the image is not lost; rather, it is distorted in its relation to God.

Bonaventure sees the effects of sin primarily in humanity's desire for equality of power with God. Grasping after the power of knowledge which only the Son of God possesses, humans fell into sin. With sin, therefore, humans became anxious seekers, desperately seeking that which they lost. Because they turned from truth and became enmeshed in ignorance, they got entangled in endless questions through curiosity. Here is where Bonaventure locates the snare of philosophy. Philosophers are constantly asking questions and begging for truthful answers that only theology can provide. Without God, truth is never found, and covetousness is never satisfied. Rather, the covetous person is entwined in endless questions and the desire for pleasurable answers.

Bonaventure's understanding of sin speaks clearly to our contemporary world, at least in the western hemisphere. With an emphasis on materialism, information gathering, success, power and prestige, there is a compulsion to strive for some, if not all, of these attractions without limit. People are working longer hours, buying more things, reading more books, and asking more questions because they are seeking that which they have lost—or at least are striving for that which they hope will bring them fulfillment. Whatever is motivating the postmodern[32] person to seek, discover and achieve, it seems to be deeply embedded within the structure of the human person. We might say that such restless seeking is bound up with the search for true identity. Yet, such frantic seeking apart from God can only lead to the illusion of the self. In many ways, it leads to a false and private self which wants to exist outside the reach of God's will and God's love, outside of reality and outside of life. Such a self cannot help being anything but an illusion. The false self is the individual entangled in selfish desires, restless and unappeased. Because this false self stifles the life of the true self there is, at the heart of it all, a disjointedness, as one is torn between the false self and the true self, frantically searching for the ground of reality, for truth, for God.

The effect of sin, according to Bonaventure, is the loss of original justice and peace because there is a loss of grace.[33] On the one hand, this loss has corrupted the whole of humanity; the effects of sin have been globally pervasive: war, violence, oppression, domination. On the other hand, each individual has, in some way, been corrupted by sin. Whether it be in one's thoughts, feelings or actions, the relationship between individuals and the world itself is vitiated. Because friendship with God has been lost, people relate to things without taking them in their proper relation to God. The human person is disordered within and without—in the human heart of darkness and in the historical world of events. And with the disordering of the human person is the disordering of the entire universe, for only in the human can the sensible world return to its origin in God.

What Bonaventure's doctrine brings to light is that sin is not merely an individual matter. Personal sin has universal consequences. This is because sin affects not only the soul but the body as well. Bonaventure writes that both men and women disobeyed God through spiritual pride and physical gluttony.[34] As long as the soul and body were truly one, so too, creation enjoyed a spiritual relationship with God. However, with sin, the soul and body became, in a sense, "separated" from one another. The arrow of division that would ultimately fragment humankind, therefore originated in the human person through sin. The soul and body of the human person no longer mediated between God and creation. Harmony was rent asunder when the soul rose up in self-centered freedom and the body rebelled against the soul in seeking pleasure for itself. Bonaventure indicates that the body had the potency to die or not to die, to rise up against the soul or obey it.

"Abandoning the soul's true good for the sake of material satisfaction, the soul became separated against its will from the body through the body's death."[35] Thus, sin became the sword that pierced the heart of humanity, severing the spirit from the body, brother from sister, the human person from the created world. Rather than being a harmonious whole, the world became fragmented into parts, entangled in the search for fulfillment, hurling in confusion toward an unknown end.

What really went awry, in Bonaventure's view, was that humanity lost its place at the center of creation. Intended to be that "otherness" of God's self-diffusing love, to stand upright amidst the symphony of creation, chanting divine glory and praise, humanity lost its centeredness, and with that center, the true knowledge of God. Yet, this knowledge was not meant to be intellectual fact but rather knowing God with the heart—a knowledge shaped by a loving experience of God, imbued with luminous wisdom. Perfect knowledge, in this way, was meant to underscore the perfection of creation.

Bonaventure was deeply aware that sin affected the deepest root of the human person—the image of God—that which distinguished the person from the rest of creation. It is the image that opens one up to God and renders to the finite person an appetite for the infinite. Once the image was distorted, so too was human freedom. It is human freedom which makes the human spirit unique, capable of commitment to absolute love, and subject to no created power but God alone. Freedom gone awry is a world gone asunder. If the image of God, that human structure that orients us to God, is at the root of sin, Bonaventure claims that sin is really directed against the Son of God who alone is equal to the Father.[36] For humans to presume themselves equal to God is an affront against the Son who alone is the perfect image of the Father, possessing all that is of the Father, and thus equal to the Father. It is the Son, the Image and Word of the Father, who is the center of life. Through sin we have entered into competition with the Word of God hoping to win the race of perfection, but the last word of life is, indeed, the Word itself. Because of sin, Bonaventure states, humanity is fallen on the ground, immersed in the things of sense and in need of being lifted up.[37] Sin has disclosed the poverty of being human.[38] It is difficult for us to think of ourselves as being poor, especially if we are materially rich. Yet, according to Bonaventure, we are poor by nature simply because we are radically dependent on God for our very existence. That is why the Word, the Son who shares equality with the Father, accepts the poverty of the human condition and even the human's self-inflicted poverty of dejection—to show that equality with God is not something to be grasped at. On the cross, it is God himself who becomes poor.[39]

To find our way back to that loving relationship with God, Bonaventure claims, we need to be made upright once more, to be reconciled with God's loving power. We cannot do this alone, however hard we try. We continue to grasp after things that are fleeting and evasive, things that offer false promises of hope and fulfillment. Only Jesus Christ, the Word made flesh, can rescue us from this path of alienation and lead us back to God. Bonaventure uses the figure of the circle to describe this path of return. A center, he claims, maintains the perfect circle of emanation and reduction [leading back].[40] However, with sin, this center is lost due to the fall of "Adam." The center can only be restored when two lines intersect at right angles; thus it is Christ crucified who becomes center and restores the circle of life to its perfect loving relationship with God.[41] Jesus Christ, the Word incarnate, is the truth of all reality—that truth made known to us in the flesh—that we may come to know the Word and love the Word who is wisdom, that we may find our way back to the Father of overflowing goodness. As the human person is created reality brought to consciousness, Christ is the human person who represents and contains in himself the entire created order. A total turning to Christ, in Bonaventure's view, can restore that original peace and justice intended for creation, and perfect us in love, which binds all together in the community of the Trinity.

Reflections

1. Do I view the body as part of God's image? If so, how do I express this image in daily life?

2. Reflect on the idea of "original justice." How is this integral to my relationship with God?

3. Spend time in prayer reflecting on Psalm 139 verses 1–17, 23. Where do I seek my identity? In God? In others? In material things? What response must I have toward others and myself?

4. In what areas of my life is my poverty, my dependence on God, most evident? How does God respond to my poverty? In what areas of my life do I refuse to turn to God? Why? What prevents me from turning fully toward God?

Notes

1. *Brev.* 2.11 (V, 229a). "Ad perfectionem universitatis debuit fieri creatura, quae hoc sensu duplici esset praedita ad cognitionem libri scriptu intus et foris, id est Sapientiae et sui operis."
2. I *Sent.* d. 4, q. 1, a. 3, concl. (I, 786b).
3. Schaeffer, "Position and Function of Man," 294.
4. *Leg. maj.* 8.1 (EM, 64).
5. Hayes, "Incarnation and Creation," 317.
6. Schaeffer, "Position and Function of Man," 310. See Schaeffer's discussion on Bonaventure's understanding of order in creation with the human person as center (295–310).
7. *Brev.* 2.9 (V, 226).
8. *Brev.* 2.9 (V, 227).
9. *Brev.* 2.10 (V, 228); IV *Sent.* d. 45, dub. 1 (V, 507); d. 49, p. 2, a. 1, q. 1 (IV, 579); d. 43, a. 1, q. 1, (IV, 451).
10. *Brev.* 7.7 (V, 289).
11. *Brev.* 2.10 (V, 228). "Ut autem conformaretur moventi per multiformitatem potentiarum, habuit multiformitatem organorum cum summa venustate et artificiositate et ductibilitate."
12. *Brev.* 7.7 (V, 289). For an interesting discussion on Bonaventure's doctrine of the soul-body relationship see Caroline Walker Bynum, *The*

Resurrection of the Body in Western Christianity, 200–1336 (New York: Columbia University Press, 1995), 247–55. Bynum's remarks on Bonaventure's understanding of this relationship are noteworthy. She writes: "These passages [on the soul and body] are especially moving because they contain one of the rare hints—in this period of individualistic spirituality—that the union of matter and form, body and soul, might also signify a gathering of community. Bonaventure says that the rising of body for union with soul is like the restoring of Christ's dead body [the church] to life and likeness with its head" (249).

13. On the microcosm-macrocosm relationship in Bonaventure's writings see James McEvoy, "Microcosm and Macrocosm in the Writings of St. Bonaventure," *S. Bonaventura* 2:309–43.

14. Hayes, "Bonaventure: Mystery of Triune God," 67, 86.

15. *Brev.* 2.4 (V, 222). Engl. trans. De Vinck, *Breviloquium*, 80. In Bonaventure's first sermon on the Assumption, he indicates that Mary's happiness would not be complete unless she was bodily assumed into heaven. "The person is not the soul; it is a composite. Thus it is established that she must be there [in heaven] as a composite, that is, of soul and body; otherwise she would not be in perfect joy." See *De assumptione B. Virginis Mariae* 1.2 (IX, 690).

16. I *Sent.* d. 3, p. 2, dub. 1 (I, 193a). Bonaventure's doctrine of the image of God relies on Augustine (*De trinitate* 14.8.11 [*PL*, 1044]) who wrote: "The soul by the very fact that it is God's image is capable of him and can be partaker of him; which so great a good is only made possible by its being his image."

17. I *Sent.* d. 3, p. 2, a. 1, q. 1 (I, 80); *M. Trin.* q.1, concl. (V, 55); *Itin.* 3.5 (V, 305).

18. See Alvin Black, "The Doctrine of the Image and Similitude in Saint Bonaventure," *Cord* 12 (1962): 270–71. For a more detailed discussion on capacity and participation see Black's masters thesis, "The Doctrine of the Image and Similitude in Saint Bonaventure," St. Bonaventure University, 1962.

19. *Hex.* 12.9 (V, 386). Engl. trans. De Vinck, *Six Days of Creation*, 177.

20. In his disputed questions on Evangelical Perfection Bonaventure writes: "No one comes to a full notion of God except through a true and proper notion of him/herself. No one rightly knows him/herself unless s/he recognizes his/her own nothingness." See *Perf. ev.* q. 1, concl. (V, 120–121). Engl. trans. J.A. Wayne Hellmann, "Poverty: the Franciscan Way to God," *Theology Digest* 22 (1974): 339. Thomas Merton makes a distinction between the false self and true self which complements Bonaventure's understanding of the image of God and relationship to God. See Thomas Merton, *New Seeds of Contemplation* (New York: New Directions Books, 1961), 35–6.

21. III *Sent.* d. 1, a. 2, q. 3, resp. (III, 29).

22. III *Sent.* d. 1, a. 1, q. 1, ad 4 (III, 11); I *Sent.* d. 1, a. 3, q. 1 & 2 (I, 38ff) for the meaning of *convenientia ordinis*; Hayes, "The Meaning of 'Convenientia' in St. Bonaventure," 74–100.

23. Hayes, "Bonaventure: Mystery of Triune God," 86–7.

24. *Leg. maj.* 13.5 (EM, 109). Engl. trans. FA:ED II, 634.

25. *Itin.* 6.7 (V, 312); Hayes, "Bonaventure: Mystery of Triune God," 86.

26. On the mimetic nature of humans, see Gil Bailie, *Violence Unveiled: Humanity at the Crossroads* (New York: Crossroad, 1995), 133–52. Bailie is a student of René Girard who has written extensively on this subject.

27. *Brev.* 2.11 (V, 229).

28. II *Sent.* prooem. (II, 1–6). "Tunc enim homo rectus est, quando intelligentia adaequatur summae veritati in cognoscendo, voluntas conformatur summae bonitati in diligendo, et virtus continuatur summae potestati in operando."

29. *Brev.* 2.11 (V, 229); 2.12 (V, 230). Engl. trans. De Vinck, *Breviloquium*, 101, 106.

30. II *Sent.* prooem. (II, 1–6). Engl. trans. Johnson, *Bonaventure*, 57.

31. See William Thompson's discussion of Karl Jasper's axial consciousness and the implications of human autonomy and self-transcendence for the Christian in his *Christ and Consciousness* (New York: Paulist Press, 1977), 19–84.

32. Postmodernism is a complex term that describes the contemporary philosophical and cultural milieu. Coined in the 1930s, the term *postmodern* is used to describe the historical transition from modernity to a period beyond modernity, namely, postmodernity. Whereas modernity emphasized objective, logical thinking, as well as a universal morality and law, postmodernism indicates there is no transcendence in reality; rather, all knowledge is derived from the self who interprets reality. Thus, there is no single, universal worldview. Postmodernism celebrates the local and particular at the expense of the universal and emphasizes a respect for difference. For an introduction to postmodernism see Stanley J. Grenz, *A Primer on Postmodernism* (Grand Rapids: William B. Eerdmans, 1996), 39–56.

33. Original justice, for Bonaventure, consists in the integral relationship of the mind and flesh. See II *Sent.* d. 33, a. 1, q. 2 (II, 75); II *Sent.* d. 19, a. 3, q. 1, concl. (II, 470). For a discussion on Bonaventure and justice, see Bonaventure Hinwood, " 'Justice' According to St. Bonaventure," *Cord* 31 (1981): 323–35.

34. *Brev.* 3.4 (V, 233).

35. *Brev.* 3.4 (V, 234). Engl. trans. De Vinck, *Breviloquium*, 119.

36. III *Sent.* d. 1, a. 2, q. 3, ad resp. (III, 29).

37. *Itin.* 4.2 (V, 306).

38. II *Sent.* prooem. (II, 1–6). Bonaventure goes so far as to say that even accidents are more dependent upon God than they are upon the substance in which they inhere. See *Hex* 4.8 (V, 350); cf. III *Sent.* d. 1, a.

2, q. 3, ad resp. (III, 29). The creature depends essentially and totally on the Creator.

39. Hellmann, "Franciscan Way," 341.

40. Hayes, "Bonaventure: Mystery of Triune God," 79–80.

41. *Hex.* 1.24 (V, 333).

Incarnation

Words are part of our everyday life. They are integral to who we are as human beings. Words express thoughts. We go about our daily lives *thinking* about various things, and each one of our thoughts shapes the person we become that day. When these thoughts are expressed as words, they reflect the content of who we are as persons. Bonaventure was captivated not simply by words but by the Word of God. This Word, as we noted previously, is the sum total of the infinite divine ideas. When the Word is expressed in a finite way, creation bursts forth and tells us something about God.

Bonaventure described an inner relationship between the inner divine reality of the Word and the reality of the world. He used the word "congruity" or "fittingness" to describe a perfect fit between the Word and the world,[1] a fit of such proportion that without the Word incarnate, the world is incomplete. The congruity between the Word and the world is made possible by the fact that not only is everything in creation a little word (of God), but there is one in creation, the human person, who is an image of the Word and, as such, is created to express the Word in a particular and unique way.[2] It is because of the human person that the world is truly "fit" to the Word of God. What makes humanity so "fitting" to the Word is that it has the ability to receive the self-gift of God into its inner depth. As we said in the last chapter, it is this Word, the exemplary Image, who fills the potential of the creative image of the human person.[3] When this image is filled, all of material and spiritual reality (which are summed up in the human person) attain a personal relationship to God. Bonaventure described the human person as the noble potency of the created order and, in light of this potential, he explored the mystery of the Incarnation.[4] While in his scholastic writings he concentrated on the hypostatic union (the two natures of Christ), in his later spiritual writings he probed deeply into the mystery of the person of Christ, and the relationship of Christ to the Trinity and creation.

Bonaventure answered the question of "who" Jesus is early on in his career. The Incarnation, he indicated, is fundamentally about the eternal Word of God who lies at the center of the Trinity. In the Incarnation the Word takes on human nature and stands at the center of creation, and, as inspired Word, dwells at the center of the spiritual life.[5] Jesus Christ, the incarnate Word, is the eternal Word come to explicit consciousness and inspired in the human heart. In one of his sermons he writes: "But in order to become perceptible to the human senses he put on the form of flesh, and the Word was made flesh and dwelt among us, and yet he remained in the bosom of the Father."[6] When the Word became flesh, the eternal Word did not *leave* the Trinity to enter humanity; rather, the Word as eternal became incarnate. The capacity of the human person to be united to God, therefore, was fulfilled in the Incarnation.

In his scholastic writings, Bonaventure devoted considerable thought to the two natures of Christ joined together in the hypostatic union. Why, he asked, did the *Word* become flesh? If the Incarnation is about the saving completion of the universe, would it not have been more fitting that God unite himself with the *entire* universe instead of a single human nature? Or perhaps a union between God and the whole human race would have been more fitting? Bonaventure examined the congruency between a personal God of love and an individual human nature. The basis for the two natures of Christ, in his view, relates to the personal relations in the Trinity. Just as the persons of the Trinity are distinguished by origin, they are related personally in such a way that they are truly one. So too, Bonaventure claims that true union takes place in an individual human nature rather than the whole human race. One divine person united to one human nature is the true union of God with one other than God who is able to receive the fullness of divine love, that is, the human person.[7] Such is the mystery of Jesus Christ.

Bonaventure described Jesus Christ as the "Tree of Life" because it is this tree onto which we (humans) are grafted in the Incarnation, and from which we draw life. In the Incarnation God draws human nature into union so as to ground it in its divine root.[8] As the mediator between God and creation, Christ is the "ark of God" because he is the eternal principle of order within creation.[9] He is the medium or center between the Father and the created world and, as such, is the fullest expression of the Father in the world. He is the hierarch or the sacred principle of creation, the one who is the source of life, light and truth.[10] Christ is the source of grace that divinely illumines and perfects created reality. Thus, Christ is the head of creation, extending his divine influence to angels, humanity and the rest of creation. He is first and last, the Alpha and Omega, because he is the Word of God through whom all things are brought into being and through whom all things find completion.

The Incarnation is so fundamental to Bonaventure's thought that his theology is described as "Christocentric." He emphasized that it is the *Word* who became flesh and not simply "God." Often, we hear the Incarnation described as "God becoming human" but Bonaventure clarifies this by affirming that it is the *Word* of God that takes on our humanity. As Timothy Johnson states, Bonaventure is a "mystic of God's Word"[11] and the reasons for this, I believe, are two-fold. First, the Word *is* the art of the Father, the expression of the Father's ideas. Thus, everything that exists in creation is grounded in the Word of God (and not in the Father or Spirit). In this way, Bonaventure sees the Word as the source and root of all created reality. Second, Bonaventure understands the entire Trinity to be focused in the Word in an exemplary way, primarily because the Word is *medium* or center of the Trinity.[12] Thus, he describes the Incarnation as the work of the Trinity insofar as the entire Trinity is focused in the Word who takes on our humanity.[13] This relationship between the

Trinity and the Incarnation becomes more prominent in Bonaventure's spiritual writings as he realizes that in Christ the whole Trinity is expressed.

One of the most profound mysteries of Christ that attracted Bonaventure is the *centrality* of the Word. As eternal Word, Christ is center of the Trinity; as incarnate Word he is center of creation; as inspired Word, he is center of the human heart. As center of the Trinity, the Word mediates between the Father (who is totally producing) and the Spirit (who is totally produced). As center, the Word has properties of both the Father and Spirit who, in relation to each other, are opposites, that is, the Word both produces (with the Father) and is produced (like the Spirit). The Word, therefore, is a coincidence of opposites—"coincidence" because the Word shares a likeness with the Father and the Spirit.[14] With the Father, the Word shares the likeness of producing since the Word, together with the Father, "produces" the Spirit through the eternal spiration of love. With the Spirit, the Word shares the likeness of receptivity to the Father's goodness. The Word, therefore, is center of unity in the Trinity.

The notion of the Word as a center (*medium)* of opposites figures prominently in the structure of Bonaventure's thought.[15] Like a good medievalist, he sees the number three (for example, the three divine persons of the Trinity) as a perfect number because it signifies two extremes united by a common center.[16] The Trinity is perfect love because of the horizontal and vertical orders of the Trinity made possible by the centrality of the Word. Similarly, the Word mediates between the Father and creation and is the center between them. Because of the central mediating position of the Word, creation can attain perfect unity with God. Without the Word as center, God would simply not be Trinity, and the world would have nothing in common with God. While the Trinity, therefore, is the ground of relationality, the Word, as a coincidence of opposites, is the ground of *unity* of relationships.

The notion of the coincidence of opposites assumes an even more prominent role as Bonaventure considers it in light of the incarnate Word. Bonaventure identifies Christ as the coincidence of opposites in such a way that this dipolar structure undergirds the mystery of Christ. In his *Soul's Journey Into God*, for example, he writes that in Christ is joined the first principle with the last, God with man, the eternal with the temporal, the most simple with the most composite, the most perfect with the lowly, the supreme, all-inclusive One with the man Jesus Christ.[17] He continues:

> Christ, the Son of God, who is the image of the invisible God by nature [is] . . . the first and the last, the highest and the lowest, the circumference and the center, the Alpha and the Omega, the caused and the cause, the Creator and the creature, that is, the book written within and without.[18]

The profound mystery of Christ that Bonaventure describes here is that he sees Christ as the coincidence of opposites not simply on a personal level (that is, between the human person and God) but on a cosmic level.[19] Everything in creation that is opposite to another is united to the other through the Word, Jesus Christ. Because every person, plant, animal and star is created through the Word and bears a relationship to the Word, every person, plant, animal and star which, on one hand, is opposite to the other is, at the same time, related to the other precisely through the Word. Ewert Cousins refers to this union of opposites as mutual affirming complementarity.[20] That is, opposites affirm one another (as opposites) precisely because they are in union with a common center, that is, the Word. Everything in the universe, therefore, that ever was and ever will be is brought into unity with God through Jesus Christ. In Christ, all opposites coincide and because they coincide in a common center, they are in union. An understanding of Christ as the coincidence of opposites can have tremendous implications for our contemporary world, especially in areas that seek a unified relationship, such as interreligious dialogue or science and religion. Such unity, as Bonaventure indicates, can be found in Christ the center.

The notion of the coincidence of opposites leads us to suspect that the reason for the Incarnation is much more profound than the reversal of sin. Bonaventure was a realist and human sin is a reality. He described original sin as a disease which infects the mind through ignorance and the flesh through concupiscence. For this reason, he states, the whole (body and soul) had to be assumed so that the whole might be healed.[21] The Word became flesh to offer himself to all, to reveal truth and to impart the grace of healing. In the Incarnation, he writes, the eternal God has humbly bent down and lifted the lowliness of our nature into unity with his own person.[22] God has come to us in a loving and personal way, making himself visible and audible so that humanity could once again be united to God and contemplate him.[23] There is no doubt that when the Word became flesh, the eternal exemplar became temporal so that humans could learn to read the book of creation once more and find their way back to God. The broken relationship with God due to sin had to be repaired by one who is truly God and truly human, and that is Jesus Christ. Thus, for Bonaventure, the Incarnation is a work of restoration. God became human in such a way that he could be known and loved, and in this knowing and loving God in Christ, we are restored in the image in which we are created.

Although for Bonaventure sin *is* a reason for the Incarnation, and redemption is truly the work of Jesus Christ, it is clear that Bonaventure did not carve in stone Anselm's idea of satisfaction, namely, that the primary reason the Word became flesh was to repay the debt due to sin. He was aware that if sin is the impediment to true relationship with God, God could have repaired the damage caused by sin in other ways. Moreover, could the most noble work of God, the Incarnation, be due *only* to the sin of humanity? Such an idea not only seems to undermine the Incarnation but it weakens the utter congruency between the Word of God, humanity and creation. For if sin is *the* reason for the Incarnation, why is the human person structured in a way finely tuned to the *Word* of God? Could not God have repaired the damage due to sin in other ways? Questions like these must have occupied Bonaventure's mind because while he recognized the Incarnation as the work of redemption, he did not limit it to this.

If one looks at the various reasons Bonaventure offers for the Incarnation, sin is the last reason for such a magnificent event. The first reason for the Incarnation, he states, is that God's infinite power, wisdom and goodness are manifested in a perfect manner. To say that divine power, wisdom and goodness are manifested in the Incarnation is to say that the Incarnation is the work of the Trinity. The power of God is the Father, the wisdom of God is the Son, and the goodness of God is the Spirit. Thus, in the Incarnation, the triune God is expressed in history. The second reason, he states, is for perfection of the universe. Since the first (principle) should be joined with the last (humanity), it is fitting that the divine Word be united to human nature. Since the entire created order is related to humanity, it finds its fulfillment in perfect glorification of humanity. By bringing the world to completion through God's personal self-communication in the Incarnation, God has also effected the perfect object for human contemplation in glory. The *last* reason for the Incarnation, Bonaventure states, is that in order to overcome the infirmity of human sin, it was necessary to have a God-man as mediator. Thus, while sin is a reason for the Incarnation it is not the primary reason.[24]

Bonaventure viewed the Incarnation as the achievement and summit of creation. In Jesus Christ, the Word incarnate, the potency that lies in humanity to receive the very personal self-communication of God is realized. The Incarnation, therefore, is the perfect realization of what is potentially embedded in human nature, that is, union with the divine. In this way, Christ and the world are not accidentally related but intrinsically connected. Stating this in another way—more central to Bonaventure's thought—the Incarnation *completes* creation.[25] If the order of creation reaches its highpoint in humanity which has the potential for union with God, that potential is fully realized in the Word incarnate.[26] Bonaventure's Christology, therefore, is a cosmic Christology, one which finds its roots in the New Testament. In the letter to the Ephesians (1:10), for example, the author writes: "All things were created through him and for him. Before anything was created, he existed . . . and he holds all things in unity." The Pauline letters describe Christ as the center of unity drawing all things back to their origin. Since the world was created for Christ (Col 1:6), it must be recapitulated or reestablished in and through him under whose power all are to be united. This "Christic" thought is explored by the Greek Fathers such as Gregory of Nyssa and Maximus the Confessor who held that Christ is the redeeming and fulfilling center of the total created universe. Christ, the Logos, belongs to the very structure of the universe.[27]

Bonaventure, we may say, revitalizes a cosmic Christology that marked the early church. The Incarnation is not the work of God to repair a defect in creation. Rather, the Incarnation is the most noble perfection of the universe and Christ is the crown and summit of creation. As he writes:

> The most noble perfection in the universe is not attained until such time as the nature that contains germs that make for the spirit (*rationes seminales*) and the nature that contains the concepts of reason (*rationes intellectuales*) and the nature that contains the archetypal designs of the world (*rationes ideales*) are united to form one single person: and this happened at the Incarnation of the Son of God.[28]

For Bonaventure, Christ is the fulfillment of the potential that lies at the heart of creation (union with God) and he is the goal to which creation is directed. As Zachary Hayes states, the Incarnation is related not only to sin but to the free loving completion of the world by God.[29] The Incarnation is the most perfect realization of the potential of humanity as well as the perfection of the universe. In Christ the created order finds its highest fulfillment. Sin is not the primary cause of the Incarnation but the excess love and mercy of God.[30] What Bonaventure brings to light (well before Duns Scotus's doctrine of the absolute primacy of Christ) is that the Incarnation is willed for its own sake and not for the sake of any lesser good. Hayes writes: "What Jesus is about is more than ridding sin. The issue of overcoming sin is a matter of overcoming all obstacles that stand in the way of the accomplishment of God's creative aim—which is the fullest possible sharing of life and love between God and creation."[31] Sin is not the primary reason for the Incarnation; rather, love is. Hayes identifies the Incarnation as the sharing of love between God and creation. It is an ordered love because where there is perfect love, there is perfect order, and where there is perfect order, there is perfect justice and peace. Bonaventure views the Incarnation, therefore, as the perfection of the entire created order (in love). In his *Sermon on the Nativity* he writes:

> It is in the Word that we discover the perfection of that greatness of heart which brings all reality to its consummation and completion, since the figure of the circle attests to the perfection of bodies both in the macrocosm and in the microcosm. . . . But this figure is not complete in the universe. Now, if this figure is to be as perfect as possible, the line of the universe must be curved into a circle. Indeed, God is simply the first. And the last among the works of the world is man. Therefore, when God became man, the works of God were brought to perfection. This is why Christ, the God-man, is called the Alpha and Omega, the beginning and the end. For this reason, as you have heard, the last of all things, namely man, is said to be first and last. The ability of human nature to be united in a unity of persons with the divine . . . is reduced to act so that it would not be a mere empty potency. And since it is reduced to act, the perfection of the entire created

> order is realized, for in that one being the unity of all reality is brought to consummation.[32]

Just as the Word is the center of the eternal, dynamic and diffusive love of God, so now that center lies at the heart of creation, filling the human potential with the love of God and thus completing the world in the perfect order of love. It is for this reason that a world without an Incarnation is an incomplete world. We must conclude, therefore, that the Incarnation is not only about sin but, even more, it is about cosmic completion. The Incarnation fulfills both redemption *and* completion. The very fact that the Incarnation has taken place means that perfection of the universe is realizable—it can be attained.

In his final years, Bonaventure emphasized the cosmic Christ as the center of the universe, of all history and time. Christ is the most noble perfection in the universe, he states, because in Christ is united divine, human and spiritual natures.[33] That is, Christ who is truly God, is truly human, and truly belongs to the universe. Christ, therefore, is the midpoint to which the entire universe is oriented. The intricate pattern of relationships between the Trinity, creation, and humanity which connect in the person of Jesus Christ indicates to Bonaventure that, in Christ, the final end of the universe has been realized. Because the Word took on our humanity and was crucified and glorified, everything in the created universe has been transformed in Christ. In one of his sermons he proclaims:

> All things are said to be transformed in the transfiguration of Christ, in as far as something in each creature was transfigured in Christ. For as a human being, Christ has something in common with all creatures. With the stone he shares existence; with the plants he shares life; with the animals he shares sensation; and with the angels he shares intelligence. Therefore all things are said to be transformed in Christ since—in

> his human nature—he embraces something of every creature in himself when he was transfigured.[34]

Yet, if Christ has indeed perfected the universe in the order of divine love, why is the world in such turmoil? Ecosystems are being destroyed, women and children are abused, and humanity on the whole thrives on violence and power. We are, therefore, impelled to question Bonaventure's Christocentric universe. Is it simply an ideal world? I believe that Bonaventure was a realist and held up the mystery of Christ precisely in view of *this* world with its sin. He believed that all creation has a destiny in God but that the fulfillment of the created world remains incomplete. I would suggest that, for Bonaventure, the problem of an incomplete universe lies not in Christ but in the human person and perhaps in all prehuman aspects of the universe. Christ is the Word through whom all things are made and in whom all things are perfected; thus, Christ is the goal. However, Christ is not only the point of perfection but he is the model and image to which the human person, who is called to spiritual perfection, is to be formed. Here the Christ mystery intersects with the mystery of the human person and, with humanity, all of creation.

The most unique capacity of the human person is that the human is created according to the image of God. While the image to which the human person is formed is that of the Trinity, the whole Trinity is focused in a particular way in the Word, Jesus Christ. The true image to which the human is created, therefore, is Jesus Christ. Throughout his spiritual writings, Bonaventure indicates that to live in Christ *is* to live in the Trinity, and to live in the Trinity is to participate in the divine network of self-giving love.[35] Thus, just as Christ has completed the universe through his life, death and resurrection, it is we who are called, in history, to help complete the universe in Christ. The basis of universal completion, for Bonaventure, rests on the human person who, created in the image of Christ, is called to physical and spiritual wholeness in Christ, thus restoring physical and spiritual wholeness in the universe. Because sin thwarts our ability to fully live in Christ, the process of growing into the image of Christ requires change, conversion and a deepening of the spirit in God, that is, it requires a movement toward new life in Christ. This is the basis of the spiritual journey. Christ becomes truly the completion of the universe when each of us is "completed" in Christ. This completion of our lives, however, and that of the universe, rests on our freedom to *act* as image of God.

The mystery that lies at the center of creation's fulfillment is the mystery of divine freedom which is integral to the essence of God as love. Creation expresses God's freedom to love. God has loved creation in such a way that the capacity to love God is grounded in freedom and, in particular, in the human person who is created to freely love God in return. God does not use force to attract love, nor does God demand love from those capable of loving. God has simply shared the gift of love in a total and unique way with one who recapitulates the whole creation, namely, the human person. In Jesus Christ, the human capacity to love God in return is realized—and this love is the glory of God. While Jesus' response in love to the Father is the fulfillment of God's glory, the mystery of Christ is not yet complete. Why? Because *we* (humanity and creation) belong to Christ; we *are* Christ, the fullness of his body. The mystery of the image to which we are created discloses itself and becomes actual in communion. It is in communion with our fellow men and women that the mystery of the interpersonal divine presence is most clearly revealed. Interpersonal communion, through Christ the center, is an image of the trinitarian communion and a participation in it. Thus, the whole creation groans aloud as it awaits the birth pangs of a new creation (Rom 8:23). Only when human persons who are created according to the image of the Word, freely cooperate with God's love by turning toward Christ, will Christ truly be the summit and completion of creation. For then, the image of God, the reflection of his glory, will be the Son, the body of Christ, expressed as Trinity, in a communion of love.

Reflections

1. Spend time praying or journaling with images of Christ as the ark between God and creation, source of grace, the center, source of light, life and truth.

2. Pray using John 13:1–9. Do I understand the Incarnation as a means to overcome sin or as a work of divine love? What does "Christ as the fullest expression of the Father in the world" mean to me? What does this invite me to do? What hinders me?

3. What areas of my life need to be redeemed, completed? Imagine God's love healing those areas.

4. Everything that is opposite is united in the Word of God. How do I relate to others who are different from me? What is the role of Christ for me in areas of opposition? What must I do today to live more fully in relationship to others?

5. Do I see the significance of my life as a Christian in relation to the work of cosmic completion? What does this mean to me?

Notes

1. Hayes, *Hidden Center*, 63.
2. Ibid., 63–7. Hayes discusses the notion of congruity in light of Bonaventure's Christology.
3. III *Sent*. d. 1, a. 2, q. 3 resp. (III, 29ff). For Bonaventure there is an inner ordering of human nature to the second divine person.
4. See "Sermon II on the Nativity of the Lord," in *What Manner of Man*, 57–75.
5. *Itin* 4.3 (V, 306); *Brev*. 4.1 (V, 241); *Hex*. 3.2–32 (V, 343–348).
6. *Red. art*. 16 (V, 323). "Sed ad hoc, quod homini sensuali fieret cognoscibile, induit formam carnis, et Verbum caro factum est et habitavit in nobis, et tamen remansit in sinu Patris."
7. III *Sent*. d. 5, a. 1, q. 2, resp. (III, 125).
8. III *Sent*. d. 6, a. 2, q. 1 resp. (III, 158).
9. *Comm. Lc*. c. 13, n. 72 (VII, 356).

10. *Itin.* 4.5 (V, 307). The notion of hierarchy for Bonaventure connotes a spiritual order. Bonaventure uses the term "hierarchy" to describe the illumination of the soul in conformity to Christ through grace. He appropriates the term from the Pseudo-Dionysius who defines hierarchy as "a sacred order, a state of understanding and an activity approximating as closely as possible to the divine" (*De coelesti hierarchia* 3.1 [*PG* 3.166.] Engl. trans. Colm Lubheid, *Pseudo-Dionysius: Complete Works* [New York: Paulist, 1987], 153). As hierarch, Christ is the one who is supremely ordered in himself and who confers order on others. Hierarchy, therefore, is God-conformity [of the soul] through the grace that comes from Christ, enabling one to attain likeness to God; *Hex.* 21.17 (V, 434). See also Hayes, *Hidden Center*, 158–160.

11. This is the title of Johnson's book.

12. See, for example, *Hex.* 9.2 (V, 372).

13. *Brev.* 4.2 (V, 242).

14. On the coincidence of opposites see Ewert Cousins, "The Coincidence of Opposites in the Christology of St. Bonaventure," *Franciscan Studies* 28 (1968): 27–46; Idem, *Coincidence of Opposites*, 131–59. Cousins argues that the logic of the coincidence of opposites is basic to Bonaventure's entire theological vision and provides a key for deciphering its inner dynamic.

15. See *Hex.* 1.14 (V, 331–332) where Bonaventure explains the uniqueness of the Word as *medium*. He writes: "This, by necessity, must be the central one [*medium*] of the persons: for if there is one who produces and is not produced and another who is produced and does not produce, there must necessarily be a central one who is produced and produces." Engl. trans. De Vinck, *Six Days of Creation*, 8.

16. Alexander Schaeffer, "The Position and Function of Man in the Created World According to Bonaventure," (Part 2) *Franciscan Studies* 21 (1962): 265. The notion of two extremes joined by a middle term is one held by Alexander of Hales. Bonaventure appropriates this idea from his teacher and declares that an intermediate reality is *necessary* for the connection and perfection of the universe.

17. *Itin.* 6.5 (V, 311).

18. *Itin.* 6.7 (V, 312). Engl. trans. Cousins, *Bonaventure*, 108–09.

19. Cousins describes three types of cosmological coincidence of opposites: 1) maximum-minimum, 2) microcosm-macrocosm, and 3) Alpha-Omega, see *Coincidence of Opposites*, 150. Cousins examines the mystery of Christ in light of the coincidence of opposites and concludes that "Christ is the model in which the universe has been made, the goal of divinization to which it is going and the vehicle by which it will make its passover" (152).

20. Ibid., 207. According to Cousins, "Bonaventure's notion of Christ the *medium* (center) implies that Christ is the center in which opposites converge and are maintained." He identifies this union of opposites in Christ the center as mutual affirming complementarity because, in the

union of opposites, although they are genuinely united, the identity of each opposite is not only unchanged but deepened.

21. *Brev.* 4.2 (V, 242).

22. "Sermon II on the Nativity of the Lord," in *What Manner of Man*, 57.

23. Bonaventure, *Vigilia nativitatis Dominis* (IX, 103a). Bonaventure states that before his birth the Word was incomprehensible but after his birth he was like a word expressed by the voice, clothed in flesh and perceptible to the senses. In the Incarnation, the Word became visible and audible so that seeing and hearing, one could come to know God.

24. For a summary of the reasons for the Incarnation, see Francis Xavier Pancheri, *The Universal Primacy of Christ*, trans. Juniper B. Carol (Front Royal, VA: Christendom Publications, 1984), 19–20; Hayes, *Hidden Center*, 172–73.

25. Zachary Hayes has written extensively on this idea. See Hayes, "Incarnation and Creation," 320–29; Idem, *Hidden Center,* 161–91; Ibid., "Christology—Cosmology," 41–58.

26. See "Sermon II on the Nativity," in *What Manner of Man*, 57–75.

27. For a discussion of the cosmic Christology of the Greek Fathers see George A. Maloney, *The Cosmic Christ: From Paul to Teilhard* (New York: Sheed and Ward, 1968), 142–81.

28. *Red. art.* 20 (V, 324). "Per similem igitur rationem potest argui, quod summa perfectio et nobilissima in universo esse non possit, nisi natura in qua sunt rationes seminales, et natura, in qua sunt rationes intellectuales, et natura, in qua sunt rationes ideales, simul concurrant in unitatem personae, quod factum est in Filii Dei incarnatione."

29. Hayes, *Hidden Center*, 163.

30. Ibid., 190.

31. Zachary Hayes, "Christ, Word of God and Exemplar of Humanity: The Roots of Franciscan Christo-centrism and Its Implications for Today," *Cord* 46.1 (1996): 9.

32. "Sermon II on the Nativity," in *What Manner of Man*, 73–4.

33. *Red art.* 20 (V, 324).

34. Bonaventure, *Dominica prima in quadragesima. Sermo* 1 (IX, 215–219); Hayes, "Christ, Word of God and Exemplar of Humanity," 13.

35. This idea lies at the heart of the last three chapters of the *Itinerarium.* See Delio, "Bonaventure's Metaphysics of the Good," 228–46.

Journey to God

The integral relationship between Christ and humanity that becomes ever more apparent to Bonaventure takes a more concrete direction in his spiritual writings. These writings which emerge after his departure from the University reveal a continuous effort to see the significance of Christ not only for Christian life but for renewal of creation itself. The model Christian who weaves in and out of these writings is, of course, Francis of Assisi. It is apparent that Bonaventure meditated on the life of Francis and came to perceive the significance of Francis's life in union with Christ. Francis is one who was rightly restored in the image of Christ and, becoming conformed to God in his own life, transformed the world around him. The journey to God, therefore, which holds up Francis as the model *viator*, recapitulates Bonaventure's thought, namely, that we come from God, we exist as the image of God, and we are returning to God.

The most apt comment one can make about Bonaventure's classic, *The Soul's Journey Into God*, is that it is the least concrete of his writings. Rather, it is a highly speculative, symbolic and mystical work that maps out the journey to God in six stages, culminating in the seventh stage of ecstatic wisdom.[1] Bonaventure uses the metaphor of journey (*iter*) to indicate that the human desire for God is dynamic and changing. It is a desire which impels one to *search* for God, and this desire, planted as a seed of grace, is already deep within the human person. Because of this desire, the human person is not simply happy or content with the totality of that which exists; rather, there is a longing for more, for something deeper, for God. The human person has an attraction for God. While this desire for the ground of one's being impels one to embark on the spiritual journey, Bonaventure also recognizes other aspects of life that are required for the journey to God. Highlighting Francis as the model, he indicates that one cannot begin the journey to God unless one recognizes one's poverty or radical dependency on God. At the beginning of the *Soul's Journey Into God*, Bonaventure writes: "Here begins the reflection of the poor man in the desert." While the "poor man" is Francis, it is, more generally, every person who is radically dependent on God. Poverty, therefore, is not simply a lack of money or things. Rather, it is an awareness of one's utter dependency on God, a realization that all good things flow out of the goodness of God. The person who is poor is conscious of God's gifts and, thus, relies on God to make the journey.

With poverty as the starting point of the journey to God, Bonaventure emphasizes that the journey is not an intellectual exercise; it is not a "head trip" but a matter of the heart. The goal of the journey is happiness and, in Bonaventure's view, one cannot be happy unless the heart is centered in God.[2] One of the greatest obstacles to the spiritual journey, he claims, is that the human heart is hardened by sin. He describes the obstinate human heart as "hard," "perverse" and "proud."[3] Such a heart, he indicates, is closed to God. To begin the journey to God, one must desire God, and to truly desire God, one must "apply the heart." For Bonaventure, this means opening up one's heart to the challenges and risks of compassionate or agapic love. The prophet Ezekiel highlights the meaning of the heart open to God when he writes: "I will give you a new heart and place a new spirit within you, taking from your bodies your stony hearts and giving you natural hearts" (Ezek 36:27). This, too, is what Bonaventure is saying: the "hardened," self-centered heart must become a natural, loving heart, centered in God. Transformation of the heart, however, can only come about through a relationship *with* God. That is why Bonaventure indicates that prayer is the mother and source of the journey to God—because prayer is an openness and deepening of one's life in God's life.[4] Prayer is that primary speech uttered within the depths of the human person—that dialogue in love between the word (human person) and the Word of God.

The journey begins on the level of creation. Originally, Bonaventure states, humanity was made fit for the quiet of contemplation, and therefore God placed humans in a paradise of delight. In this original paradise the human person was endowed with a "triple eye": the eye of the flesh, of reason, and of contemplation.[5] According to Bonaventure, the eye of the flesh was created to see the things outside in creation, the eye of reason to see things within, and the eye of contemplation to see things above.[6] Originally, the human eye saw that creation is good and sacred; it is like a river which flows from God. It is replete with the power, wisdom and goodness of God, and every level of creation is a mirror reflecting the triune God. Creation has a sacred purpose, and that is to awaken the human spirit to God—to love, praise, reverence and give thanks. The human person, in Bonaventure's view, is to be immersed in reverent contemplation of the world, not to flee it, but to embrace it, so as to be drawn to its source who is God.[7] Bonaventure describes creation as a theophany, a manifestation of God. Creation signifies the overflowing goodness of God in the myriad life-forms of creation. The simple order and beauty of creation can enkindle the human heart to long for God because every aspect of creation is like a reflecting pool of the divine.

Despite the beauty and wisdom of creation, Bonaventure claims, humans became blinded to its beauty and ignorant of its meaning. Sin distorted the triple eye of the human person in such a way that the beauty and wisdom of creation became obscure. Throughout his writings, Bonaventure uses vivid symbols to paint a picture of the human person in the tragic state of sin. He speaks of the human person as having fallen and lying on the ground in need of a helping hand to raise the human person up.[8] He describes a strange blindness of the intellect which prevents the human from seeing the presence of God.[9] Accustomed to darkness of sensation, the human person is like a bat in the daylight that sees nothing.[10] Blinded and bent over, sitting in darkness, the human "does not see the light of heaven unless grace with justice comes to one's aid against concupiscence and unless knowledge with wisdom comes to one's aid against ignorance. All this is done through Jesus Christ."[11] It is Christ alone who restores the true light of knowledge so that the beauty of creation may be seen in its proper relation to God and, indeed, may lead us to God.

Although the book of creation is illegible to the human person wandering about in darkness, Bonaventure indicates that the created world can impart to the human person a certain knowledge of God. The beauty, order, wisdom and goodness of creation signifies that there must be One who is beautiful, orderly, wise and good, and this is God. Because the knowledge that comes from creation is limited, the human person who desires God is impelled to seek a deeper knowledge of God, and this knowledge is within. The human person who is finite cannot know God who is infinite, unless s/he finds a true ground of relationship. Since the created world is finite, one must enter within the human soul created in the image of God which has the capacity for the infinite God. It is here that one finds a ground of loving relationship with God. Thus, if one begins the journey to God on the level of creation and is inspired to seek God more deeply, one is impelled to search within where God dwells deep within the center of the soul. The degree to which one enters into this relationship, however, depends on how open one is to knowing God and to knowing oneself in God. That is, one who truly desires God must be ready to encounter the Truth. This is the knowledge, according to Bonaventure, that not only forms a deep relationship with God but, moreover, leads to true love of God. Knowledge and love are the rings of the ladder by which one ascends to God.

The question of *how* we know God and the things of God has been a source of philosophical study for eons. Aristotle claimed that the basis of all knowledge is the external world by which we come to knowledge of things through the five human senses (touch, taste, sight, smell, hearing). The influx of this sensory knowledge, according to Aristotle, is the basis of human knowledge. While Bonaventure did not entirely refute Aristotle's idea of knowledge, he did not believe that the soul is a *tabula rasa* waiting to receive information through the senses so that it could translate it into bits of knowledge; that is, the entirety of our knowledge does not come from the external world.[12] Rather, he believed that there is a light within the human soul that enables one to know things with certainty; it is a divine light which illuminates the truth of things and allows one to judge the certitude of things. The human mind, therefore, is not merely a blank tablet on which concepts are inscribed, but a mirror that is turned to the radiating light of the divine essence, a light which shines within the soul and penetrates one's whole being. In fact, it is because of this light that humans have knowledge of things they have never experienced through the senses, for example, infinity, virtue, or justice. Following Augustine, Bonaventure held that within the human soul are eternal reasons (*rationes aeternae*) that enable the human person to know the truth of God, and the truth of all things in God. It is an inner light "from above" that shines on the human soul and illumines it (thus, the "doctrine of illumination").[13] It is the light of truth that regulates and motivates human reason and enables one to know things as true and certain.

Although Bonaventure's doctrine of illumination is a classical (Augustinian) idea and would probably be dismissed by contemporary scientists as "medieval," still, it offers an explanation of how we know the truth of things in God. It is a doctrine of knowledge that is grounded in relationship to God. In our modern age we hold up knowledge as an end in itself, but for Bonaventure knowledge is to bring us to the truth of things as they exist in relation to God. That is, knowledge is not an end in itself; it is a means to God. And it is to lead one ultimately to the love of God.[14] To come to this knowledge, Bonaventure states, we must enter within, that is, we must move ever more closely to the divine light which radiates within us, illuminating the truth of our lives and the truth of the world around us. The problem of turning within, however, and turning toward this light, is that we are bound by sin.

Sin, as we said before, darkens the intellect, enslaves one in the things of the senses, and impels one to wander in the world aimlessly, asking endless questions, seeking that which was lost. Bonaventure writes: "It seems amazing . . . that God is so close to our souls that so few should be aware of the first principle within themselves."[15] Although we have a human nature fitting (or congruent) to God being created in his image, and we have a desire for God awakened by the created world and sustained by grace, we are simply unable to turn fully toward God because of sin. The root of sin lies in the fact that the human person is created in the image of God. Not that we are inherently sinful. We are created in the goodness of God, according to Bonaventure, but the very fact that we are *created* means that we have limited freedom and not perfect freedom as God possesses. Perfect freedom is rooted in perfect love and can choose nothing other than perfect love. Limited freedom means we can choose other than perfect love, that is, we have the ability to turn away from God and choose something other than God—and this is the root of sin. To be an image of God, therefore, is both the source of human perfection and human tragedy; for the divine image is a fallen image. Instead of being upright, turned toward God, the human is entangled in infinite questions, and this means searching for that lost contact with God. Fallen into a fragmented world with a thousand desires, a thousand questions, the human is like dust driven by the wind of desire for that which is lost—for God. This is source of human anxiety, restlessness and suffering. The human mind, Bonaventure writes, "is distracted by cares, clouded by sense images, allured by concupiscense, and thus totally lying in the things of sense."[16] We are simply unable to enter within as *into the image of God.*

The lack of interiority, which Bonaventure highlights here, is becoming increasingly apparent in our contemporary culture which is media-saturated. We are so bombarded by a steady stream of visual and auditory images that we are becoming conditioned to sensory overload. Television, telephones, movies and internet have all made us so dependent on incoming sensory information that, apart from these media sensations, we are restless and bored. We are losing the ability to enjoy solitude and to be at peace within ourselves. Yet, the key to finding fulfillment, according to Bonaventure, is by entering into the image of God. "God is the One who is closer to you than you are to yourself," Bonaventure writes.[17] The problem of recognizing the nearness of God, however, is that sin makes us anxious and restless. We are so entangled "without" that we find it difficult to enter "within." One of the attractions of New Age spirituality is that it promotes "withinness" by emphasizing inner peace, mind-body harmony, inner control—things that promote the wholeness of the human person. While these things are good in themselves, they can also give rise to an extreme self-centeredness if they are not held in proper relation to God. Only when God, the image in whom we are created, is the basis of the human spiritual quest, is the fullness of happiness and peace attained.

Because humanity lies fallen on the ground, Bonaventure states, it needs help in rising from the things of sense to see itself (truthfully) and the Eternal Truth in itself. This help comes to us in Jesus Christ who, as Word, is the Truth of all reality. It is Christ who restores the ladder of relationship to God.[18] Any knowledge apart from Christ, according to Bonaventure, will ultimately be futile. As he writes: "No matter how enlightened one may be by the light of natural and acquired knowledge, s/he cannot enter into him/her self . . . unless Christ be his/her mediator."[19] Bonaventure crystallizes the path to true knowledge by stating that Christ is the way, the truth and the life. Christ is the door to knowledge, and to enter through this door one must believe in Christ, hope in him, and love him. True knowledge, therefore, is based on faith, hope and love in God who is enfleshed in Jesus Christ. Yet, the type of knowledge to which Bonaventure is referring is not "book" knowledge; rather, it is knowledge that emerges through relationship with Christ. One cannot enter into the mystery of God apart from a deeply personal relationship with Christ. That is why devotion to Christ is pivotal in the journey to God; how one relates to Christ will influence how one completes the journey, that is, whether or not one will arrive at the goal of the journey which is union with God. For Bonaventure there is no union with God (that is, contemplation) apart from Christ. Devotion to the humanity of Christ is to lead to the contemplation of God.

In our contemporary age which is witnessing a resurgence of devotion to Christ, it is helpful to understand how someone like Bonaventure who promoted this devotion, understood its meaning and purpose. For Bonaventure, devotion to Christ means a total turning to Christ, not simply with one's mind but with one's heart and soul as well.[20] Such devotion is intended to develop a personal relationship with a personal God of love, revealed in the life, death and resurrection of Jesus Christ. In light of Bonaventure's writings, I would describe devotion to the humanity of Christ as affective, mystical and transformative. As we said previously, relationship with God must be first and foremost a matter of the heart. If one truly seeks a relationship with God, one must "apply the heart" through prayer, asceticism, and loving relationships. For Bonaventure, true relationship with God means developing a real, loving relationship with Christ through prayer, meditation and contemplation.[21] Christ is the mediator between God and humanity and the one in whom God is revealed. Thus, accepting Christ as person and developing a personal relationship with Christ ultimately opens us up to the mystery of God.

Bonaventure was aware, however, that such a relationship is not easy because of our fallen human nature. He, therefore, composed a work entitled *The Tree of Life*, to foster this devotion. It is a work based on the gospels but structured in such a way that the harmony of the gospels forms a story of the life of Jesus Christ. The work is comprised of a series of meditations, each of which uses the senses and imagination to engage the reader in the life of Christ. Such an approach, in

Bonaventure's view, should transform the hardened human heart into one of compassionate love. Bonaventure, we might say, is very "holistic" in his approach to God. In his view the whole person must encounter the whole Christ. Even on the human level, a heart opened to another comes to know the other on the level of the senses as well as the spirit. There is no true spiritual love apart from the physical senses. Relationship with God, therefore, is confined neither to the head nor to the heart but emerges out of a true union of these centers as they are directed to Christ in knowledge and love. True love of God can never be attained apart from experiencing that divine love as it is given to us in Christ. This is the purpose of devotion to the humanity of Christ—to experience God.

The experience of God as Bonaventure describes it is an experience that begins with the senses. In the *Tree of Life* he uses words such as "imagine," "remember," "search," "rejoice," "receive"—words of sensible action that impel the believer to engage in Christ's life so as to become one with him.[22] For example, in a meditation entitled "Jesus Tempted by the Enemy," Bonaventure urges the reader to join with Christ in the desert because only in union with Christ can we overcome the challenges of sin so as to be turned more fully to God. He writes:

Come now, disciple of Christ,
Search into the secrets of solitude with your loving teacher,
so that having become a companion of wild beasts,
you may become an imitator and sharer
of the hidden silence,
the devout prayer, the daylong fasting
and the three encounters
with the clever enemy.[23]

For Bonaventure, Christ is the source of grace by which the soul is purified, illumined and perfected.[24] As one enters more deeply into relationship with Christ, the divine image is reformed and restored in its likeness to God. Bonaventure uses the term "hierarchy" to indicate that in union with Christ, the soul is "reordered."[25] The word "hierarch," as we indicated before, means "sacred" (*hier*) "principle" (*arche*). Christ is the "sacred principle" or hierarch who restores the soul to its God-conformed likeness; the more God-like the soul becomes by grace, the more clearly it sees the truth of things, that is, the more it is illumined. Bonaventure states, "the soul [then] believes and hopes in Jesus Christ and loves him, who is the incarnate, uncreated and inspired Word—the way, the truth and the life."[26] Rather than restlessness and anxiety holding a grip on one's being, one's inner life becomes more orderly and peaceful; charity is set in order, as Augustine once said. While Bonaventure's language of hierarchy may deter us from grasping the deeper significance of relationship with Christ, it is important to keep in mind that what he is highlighting is the interior ordering of the soul. That is, when our feelings, thoughts, emotions (and other internal powers) are rightly ordered to God, then we start to live in a new, virtuous way that follows the example of Christ. Not only does the grace-filled interior ordering of our lives lead us to greater "God-likeness" but our relationship to God within continues to deepen. We begin to see truth more clearly—the truth of God and the truth of our lives in God. And the deepening of our lives in truth is, at the same time, a deepening of love in union with God, that is, with the God who reveals himself to us in Christ. As the soul is made hierarchical in Christ, it becomes the dwelling place of the Trinity. It is made a daughter of the Father, a spouse of Christ, and a temple of the Holy Spirit.[27] In union with Christ, therefore, one enters, mystically, into the life of the Trinity.

Bonaventure further explores this interior reordering by saying that, as one enters more fully into relationship with Christ, one's spiritual senses are recovered. In this way, the presence of God is truly experienced within. As he writes:

> When by faith the soul believes in Christ as the uncreated Word and Splendor of the Father, it recov-

> ers its spiritual hearing and sight: its hearing to receive the words of Christ and its sight to view the splendors of Light. When it longs in hope to receive the inspired Word, it recovers through desire and affection the spiritual sense of smell. When it embraces in love the Word incarnate, receiving delight from him and passing over into him through ecstatic love, it recovers its sense of taste and touch.[28]

The doctrine of the spiritual senses is one favored by the Fathers of the Church. Origen, Gregory of Nyssa and Augustine all spoke of an interior experience of God through the spiritual senses. Bonaventure renews this doctrine but in a way integral to his devotion to the humanity of Christ. He points out that when the soul recovers these spiritual senses, it can fully embrace the God of compassionate love, and then the soul is prepared to ascend the heights of ecstatic contemplation.

If devotion to Christ is affective, it is equally mystical. In his meditations, Bonaventure emphatically points out that relationship with Christ is not some heart-warming human experience. Rather, it is relationship with God and, as he points out frequently in his writings, it is relationship with a God who has loved us precisely through suffering and dying on the cross. Bonaventure warns his readers at the beginning of the *Tree of Life* that they are not to think of Jesus in any way less than God. He writes: "When you hear that Jesus is begotten of God, beware lest some inadequate thought of the flesh appear before your mind's eye."[29] In his meditations on the birth of Jesus, he exhorts his readers to "adore, confess, and praise this humble God lying in a manger."[30] To think of Christ as merely human is to miss the hiddenness of God present in the human form of Jesus Christ. Bonaventure never tired of pointing out this mystery and often quoted Isaiah (45:15), "truly, you are a hidden God."[31] To those covered by the darkness of sin and entangled in questions, the hiddenness of God is inscrutable; however, to those in whom grace has unveiled the inner light, the hiddenness of God is revealed in the poor and humble Christ. Perhaps Bonaventure was inspired here by Francis himself who, in his writings, frequently highlighted the humility of God. In his *Letter to the Entire Order*, for example, Francis writes:

Let everyone be struck with fear,
let the whole world tremble,
and let the heavens exult
when Christ, the Son of the living God,
is present on the altar in the hands of a priest!
O wonderful loftiness and stupendous dignity!
O sublime humility!
O humble sublimity!
The Lord of the universe,
God and the Son of God,
so humbles Himself
that for our salvation
He hides Himself
under an ordinary piece of bread!
Brothers, look at the humility of God,
and *pour out your hearts before Him!*[32]

Francis was keenly aware that the truly humble God was present in Jesus Christ, and he had a firm word of exhortation to those who did not believe, saying that those who do not see and believe are lost.[33] Francis, therefore, like Bonaventure, proclaimed that only the humble can enter into the humble love of God. And this entering into God begins with devotion to Christ because the turning of one's whole being to Christ opens one up to the mystery of God.

Finally, devotion to Christ must ultimately be transformative. It must lead the believer ever more deeply into the truth of Christ who is the Word of God. Entering into this truth enables one to know the truth of oneself and the truth of God. The Franciscan penitent and mystic, Angela of Foligno, claimed that union with Christ impelled her to recognize her nothingness or poverty before God. At the same time, however, one must come to recognize the totality of one's life in God. Truth leads to a relationship in love whereby one's life becomes totally centered in God. The hardened heart becomes the compassionate heart, and the mind, flooded by the divine light, knows itself as truly belonging to God. In Bonaventure's view, this is the basis of contemplation because through transformation in Christ the triple eye of the human person is restored. One sees the truth of all reality, and in seeing rightly one loves rightly. Personal relationship with Christ orients one to a deeper love of God, neighbor, and the surrounding created world, and this deepening of love must be expressed in one's actions. Devotion to Christ is the basis of a transformed world, therefore, because only love and the grace that comes from Christ can convert the darkness of matter into the light of the spirit.

Bonaventure's description of the soul's journey to God is thoroughly Christocentric since Christ is the beginning, middle and end of the journey. What is easily overlooked in this journey to God, however, is that it cannot be made apart from the imitation of Christ. While the journey is interior, it is not limited to the soul alone. Rather, it is a journey that encompasses the whole of the human person, body and soul. Just as the eternal Word is the expression of the Father, so too, the Word incarnate is the expression of God and, therefore, Jesus Christ is not only the interior teacher of the soul but the exemplar and model of human action. There is no journey to God, in Bonaventure's view, that does not ultimately transform the entire person. Thus, whatever takes place inwardly must express itself outwardly. While the goal of the journey is contemplation, Bonaventure clearly points out that Christ is the mediator and door by which one enters into contemplation of God, and contemplation of the world in God. For Bonaventure, contemplation is not an ascent of the soul to the uncreated divine Word in a purely intellectual manner. Rather, contemplation takes place in imitation of Christ. Although imitation of Christ is not usually the way we think of contemplation, in Bonaventure's view, it is what makes the harmony of the universe complete, because contemplation enables one to see with perfect clarity; and when we see clearly, so too do we love rightly. As Angela of Foligno professed, "as we see so we love. The more perfectly and purely we see, the more perfectly and purely we love."[34] It is love, vivified by the power of the Spirit, that binds all together in the unity of the Father and Son. Thus, where there is unity of love, there is the Trinity, and where there is the Trinity, there is happiness and peace. For Bonaventure this is the goal of the journey—happiness and peace.

Reflections

1. Has your understanding of God changed over the course of your life? How has it changed? If not, why not?

2. Spend time reflecting on your life. In praying, consider those times in which you felt you reflected God's love; those times you were crucified; those times you felt to be in the desert or tomb. How do you view your journey to God in terms of conversion?

3. Do you desire God? If not, what is hindering you? How do you express your desire for God?

4. Pray or journal using John 21:15–19. Where is your heart? Is it hardened or open to the challenges and risks of compassionate love? How would you respond to the question, "do you truly love me"?

Notes

1. For a discussion on Bonaventure's use of symbols in the *Soul's Journey Into God,* see Ambrose Nguyen Van Si, "The Journey-Symbols in St. Bonaventure's *Itinerarium,*" *Greyfriars Review* 9.3 (1995): 309–30; Bernard McGinn, "Ascension and Introversion in the *Itinerarium Mentis in Deum,*" vol. 3, *S. Bonaventura*, 535–52.

2. It is worth noting that, at the beginning of his *Soul's Journey,* Bonaventure clearly indicates that the journey is, ultimately, in the pursuit of happiness. He writes: "Since happiness is nothing other than the enjoyment of the highest good and since the highest good is above, no one can be made happy unless s/he rise above her/himself, not by an ascent of the body, but of the heart." Engl. trans. Cousins, *Bonaventure,* 59.

3. The biblical idea of the heart as the spiritual center of the human person was a common theme throughout the Middle Ages. Bonaventure uses the word in the traditional fashion whereby the heart is the seat of intelligence and love, with a special emphasis on the affective aspect. See Jean Châtillon, *Dictionnaire Spiritualité* 2:2289–2300. See especially col. 2298 for Bonaventure's use of this term.

4. *Itin.* 1.1 (V, 297).

5. *Brev.* 2.12 (V, 230).

6. *Brev.* 2.12 (V, 230).

7. Paul Rout, *Francis and Bonaventure* (Ligouri, MO: Triumph Books, 1997), 41–3.

8. *Itin.* 4.2 (V, 306).

9. *Itin.* 5.4 (V, 309).

10. *Itin.* 5.4 (V, 309).

11. *Itin.* 1.7 (V, 298).

12. For Bonaventure's views on knowledge and Christ in light of Aristotle and Plato see his sermon "Christ, the One Teacher of All," in *What Manner of Man,* 37.

13. Bonaventure *Quaestiones disputatae de scientia Christi* 4 (V, 24a). Engl. trans. Zachary Hayes, *Disputed Questions on the Knowledge of Christ,* vol. 4, *Works of Saint Bonaventure,* ed. George Marcil (St. Bonaventure, NY: The Franciscan Institute, 1992), 55–9; Black, "Doctrine of the Image and Similitude," 271; M. Hurley, "Illumination According to Bonaventure," *Gregorianum* 32 (1951): 388–404.

14. In his sermon "Christ, the One Teacher of All," Bonaventure places knowledge in the service of contemplation which he describes as wisdom. He writes: "It is clear by what order and by which author we are to arrive at wisdom. The order is this: that we begin with the firmness of faith and proceed through the serenity of reason so as to arrive at the sweetness of contemplation." The "author" to whom he is referring is Christ. Without faith in Christ, knowledge can lead one astray—this is the problem, according to Bonaventure, with the "pagan" philosophers. See "Christ, the One Teacher of All," in *What Manner of Man*, 34–5.

15. *Itin*. 4.1 (V, 306). Engl. trans. Cousins, *Bonaventure*, 87.

16. Ibid.

17. *Soliloquium de quatuor mentalibus exercitiis* 1.5 (VIII, 31). Engl. trans. José de Vinck, "Soliloquy," in *Mystical Opscula*, vol. 3, *Works of Bonaventure* (Paterson, New Jersey: St. Anthony Press, 1966), 44. Bonaventure's thought here is based on that of Augustine who wrote:

"You were more intimately present to me than my innermost self, and superior to my highest being" (Augustine *The Confessions*, transl. by Maria Boulding, O.S.B. [Hyde Park, NY: New City Press, 1997] 83).

18. *Itin.* 4.2 (V, 306).

19. Ibid. Engl. trans. Cousins, *Bonaventure,* 88.

20. In his sermon *De Sancti M. Magdalena* 3 (IX, 561a) Bonaventure describes devotion as the affection of grateful love arising from the remembrance of the benefits of Christ.

21. *Itin.* 1.8 (V, 298). For a discussion on prayer in Bonaventure, see Timothy Johnson, *Iste pauper clamavit: Saint Bonaventure's Mendicant Theology of Prayer*, vol. 390, European University Studies (Frankfurt am Main: Peter Lang, 1990).

22. Bonaventure's *Tree of Life* (*Lignum vitae* [hereafter *Lig.vit.*]) belongs to the genre of the *vitae Christi* tradition characterized by the gospel harmony, a type of meditation popular in the thirteenth century. Gospel harmonies were structured in such a way that the listener/reader could use the senses and imagination to envision the course of Christ's earthly life and achieve a type of *imitatio* that would lead to penance and conversion. On gospel harmonies, see Denise Depres, *Ghostly Sights: Visual Meditation in Late-Medieval Literature* (Norman: Pilgrim Books, 1989), 24–54.

23. *Lig. vit.* 10 (V, 73). Engl. trans. Cousins, *Bonaventure,* 134.

24. *Itin.* 4.3 (V, 306).

25. *Itin.* 4.4 (V, 307).

26. *Itin.* 4.3 (V, 306). Engl. trans. Cousins, *Bonaventure,* 89.

27. *Brev.* 5.1 (V, 252).

28. *Itin.* 4.3 (V, 306). Engl. trans. Cousins, *Bonaventure*, 89; Karl Rahner "The Doctrine of the 'Spiritual Senses' in the Middle Ages," in *Experience of the Spirit: Source of Theology*, trans. David Morland, vol. 16, *Theological Investigations* (New York: Seabury Press, 1979), 104–34.

29. *Lig. vit.* 1 (VIII, 71). Engl. trans. Cousins, *Bonaventure,* 126.

30. *Lig. vit.* 6 (VIII, 72).

31. "Sermon II on the Nativity," in *What Manner of Man*, 60.

32. Francis of Assisi "A Letter to the Entire Order" 26–27. Engl. trans. FA:ED I, 118.

33. See Francis's first Admonition (1.8), in FA:ED I, 41.

34. *Angela of Foligno: Complete Works*, 242.

Imitation of Christ

The journey to God is really a journey in love deepened by knowledge of God that, in Bonaventure's thought, finds its deepest meaning in the imitation of Christ. While the imitation of Christ as described in the Pauline letters and in the popular work by Thomas à Kempis means discipleship, it was never intended to be a superficial imitation of the actions of Christ. There is a tendency today to disparage the idea of imitating Christ because the idea of imitating a Jewish male figure from Palestine seems antithetical to feminist consciousness and pluralism. However, the meaning of imitating Christ is more than what "meets the eye"; rather, it has theological implications that are integral to the significance of being Christian. The importance of imitating Christ, in Bonaventure's view, is that by becoming Christ-like, one passes over in Christ into the mystery of the Father. Imitation, therefore, is much more profound than simply asking, "what would Jesus do?"[1] Rather, the depths of imitation correspond to transformation in grace, a new life in the spirit and the expression of this new life in one's actions and deeds. Imitation, as we said before, relates to the word "image." To imitate is to image.[2] It is not meant to be a literal mimicking of actions but has the deeper meaning of expressed likeness. The notion of expression which is integral to Bonaventure's theology is rooted in the Word of God. When the Word becomes flesh, the perfect image of the Father is expressed in history and time. Christ's humanity is the sacrament of God. In a similar way, by imitating Christ, one becomes the expressed likeness of Christ through a transformation in grace. That is, the human person becomes the sacrament of God.

Imitation, we might say, is a life-long journey of becoming a true "icon" of God. As image of God we are created in such a way as to imitate God. Just as the Word imitates the Father as expressed likeness, so too we are formed in a way congruent to the Word with the capacity to imitate (image) the Word. The imitation of Christ is sacramental in such a way that God becomes truly present in the world through our lives. Since it mediates the conscious presence of God among us, imitation cannot be abstract. Rather, it involves both the content of the image and the form in which the image is expressed; thus, imitation is manifested in action.[3] Simply put, what a person is in their interior "image" is how a person appears or expresses oneself exteriorly—a distorted image yields a sinful disposition. For example, a person who is angry interiorly expresses that anger exteriorly in various ways: rudeness, disrespect, or physical violence. Conversely, a person who is rooted in God and at peace interiorly expresses peace exteriorly through gentleness, self-control, patience and love. These examples, reshaped in the various experiences of our lives, indicate that one's interior relationship to God bears its effects exteriorly, in one's relations to others and to creation.

Bonaventure maintained that the expressed Word in creation, Jesus Christ, is the divine-temporal exemplar. As the divine exemplar, the Word is the archetype or model of everything that exists; as the temporal exemplar, he is the mirror of all graces, virtues, and merits and every creaturely attitude before God.[4] Bonaventure clearly distinguished between those actions of Christ that are to be imitated and those that are not. He states that imperfect acts directed toward the weak do not always have to be imitated and in some circumstances it is better not to imitate them (for example, walking on water!). On the other hand, no restrictions are placed on the imitation of those actions of Christ, such as prayer, which directly concern the perfection of life in Christ.[5] With this in mind, Bonaventure holds up the form of Christ's life in poverty and humility as the most perfect form of imitation and identifies the true expressed image of God in the cross of Jesus Christ.

For centuries, Franciscans have been arguing over poverty. Even in Bonaventure's time the dispute between the mendicants and secular masters at the University of Paris was concerned with the issue of poverty. The mendicants claimed to follow the poor and humble Christ while the secular masters charged them with violating their ideal. Bonaventure defended the Franciscan ideal of poverty both in his *Disputed Questions on Evangelical Perfection* and his *Defense of the Mendicants*. What Bonaventure brought to light in these works is that the spiritual significance of poverty and humility corresponds to the imitation of Christ. Humility (not poverty), he claimed, is the root and guardian of all other virtues.[6]

Although Bonaventure does not trace humility to its origin in the Trinity, it is possible to identify its trinitarian roots in light of his understanding of Jesus Christ. The ground of humility can be ultimately traced to the Father. The notion of God the Father as "humble" may seem contrary to the understanding of the Father as "powerful." However, God's power is God's humble love. Only a God who can love another so completely without dominating the other or absorbing the other can be powerful, precisely as love that is humble.[7] Describing the omnipotence of God in light of the mystery of the cross, Walter Kasper writes: "It requires omnipotence to be able to surrender oneself and give oneself away; and it requires omnipotence to be able to take oneself back in the giving and preserve the independence and freedom of the recipient."[8] The humility of the Father is integral to the nature of the Father as self-diffusive goodness. Because the Father is totally self-communicative, the Father is totally turned toward the Son. What the Father *is,* is being absolutely for the other, being turned toward the other by nature of the good—this is the Father's humility. Understanding the humility of the Father helps us understand the humility of the Son who, as Word and Image, is the perfect expression of the Father. The humility of the Father is expressed in the humility of the Son who seeks in obedience to carry out the will of the Father. Christ in his human existence externalizes the eternal mystery of sonship so that the humanity of Christ is not a second word related to the inner Word but it is precisely the *form* the inner

Word takes when it is expressed externally.[9] The turning of the Father toward the Son is expressed concretely in the humility of Christ in such a way that the human mind does not grasp the hiddenness of God in Christ. As Bonaventure states, "reason fails."[10] In his meditations on the birth of Jesus, Bonaventure emphasizes the humility of God from the moment of Jesus' birth, describing the manger scene as the birth of the "humble God," the "humble Savior," the "humble king."[11] Concerning the Incarnation, he writes, "the eternal God has *humbly* bent down and lifted the lowliness of our nature into unity with his own person."[12] Christ, as the teacher of perfect humility, shows us that it is in the humbling of self that the height of imitation lies—not as passive recognition or acceptance of oppression—but that self-humbling that leads to truth and the experiential knowledge of one's own reality.[13] For Bonaventure, humility is what ultimately formed Francis into the likeness of Christ because Francis's life was totally turned to God in his conformity to Christ, and this likeness was expressed in the Stigmata.[14]

While humility is the foundation of one's life in God, it is complemented by and joined to poverty. Just as the Father is the "root" of the humility of God, so too the mystery of the Father is the ground of poverty. The poverty of the Father is expressed in the total self-gift of the Father to the Son. The Father, we might say, gives everything away. Although Bonaventure does not explicitly examine the poverty of the Father, the very mystery of the Father as self-communicative goodness and fountain-fullness allows us to speculate that the Father is the ground of both emptiness and fullness. As self-diffusive goodness, the Father communicates goodness to the Son, and because whatever the Father gives is given totally, we can describe this communication as self-gift. However, as the unbegotten infinite abyss of goodness, the Father is fountain-fullness. Only in union with the Father, therefore, is poverty both emptiness and fullness.

For Bonaventure, human poverty is rooted in existence as creature. The very fact that we exist and that we did not bring our own existence into being means that we are radically dependent on another. Life begins in the desert because we are created *ex nihilo* (out of nothing) and are essentially dependent on God.[15] The truly poor person lives in receptivity to the gift of God's overflowing goodness. The problem with humanity, Bonaventure claims, is that humans refused radical dependency on God. They desired to possess rather than accept the poverty of createdness, and this grasping after equality with God is the source of sin. Because human sin is directed against the Son who alone is equal to the Father, it is the Son who accepts the poverty of the human condition to show us that equality with God is not to be grasped at.[16]

We might put Bonaventure's understanding of poverty in the context of "true" poverty and "false" poverty. In our modern western world of economic success, poverty connotes economic and material deprivation. It is a negative, an absence of things. The economically poor person is disparaged and marginalized. The truly poor person, that is, one who is spiritually poor and who may live materially poor, recognizes the need for God in every aspect of life. The person of true poverty is one who, simply waking up in the morning to a new day, recognizes it as a gift of God and offers thanksgiving. Those living in false poverty, however, live in the illusion of never having enough. Many of us, although living economically prosperous lives, live in false poverty. It is the lie of believing that we need more to be happy. We never have enough of anything and not simply material things, but things such as more control, more power, more pleasures—things that we believe, if we possess, will make us truly happy. Those of us living in false poverty live with a sense of absence in our lives. We accumulate things, run after pleasures, seek more control and power, hoping that any or all of these things will relieve our "poverty." The paradox of our times is that the false poverty of materialism is fostering isolationism and loneliness; the more we strive for (material) things the more we are prevented from recognizing our true poverty or radical dependency on God and on others. Steeped in false poverty, we are separated further and further from God and neighbor. False poverty, we might say, is at the heart of spiritual starvation in our postmodern world. In Bonaventure's view, we are not to avoid poverty, that is, true poverty, but to embrace it and to recognize it as our need for God. It is poverty together with humility that deepens our relationship with God.

For Bonaventure, the poor and humble Christ is the truly human one whose example enables us to be restored in a right, loving relationship with God. Poverty becomes manifest in the historical career of Jesus and is expressed in the naked figure on the cross who invites us to follow him, placing our absolute trust in God alone.[17] On the cross, it is God himself who becomes poor. The emphasis that Bonaventure places on the crucified Christ cannot be overstated. The cross is perhaps the most difficult aspect of his thought and, yet, the hinge upon which the entire structure of his thought is based. The significance of the cross for Bonaventure lies in the fact that the suffering figure on the cross is *God for us.* The dereliction of the cross is the intense revelation of divine humility, and the piercing of the human heart of Christ is the opening to humanity of the depth of divine love embodied in the love of the incarnate Son.[18] The mystery of the cross, therefore, is the mystery of poverty because here God is not possessing but fully communicating the mystery of love in his radical openness to and acceptance of humanity. The cross reveals who God is—the fullness of compassionate love freely given to the other because love, by its nature, gives itself away. The sinfulness of humanity, in Bonaventure's view, is that it has failed to embrace the compassionate love of God because it has failed to grasp the significance of the cross of Jesus Christ. In our age the cross has been viewed as an instrument of oppression, especially among women and poor people who have been told to endure their sufferings in silence "like Jesus"; thus, it has become a negative aspect of Christian life. However, Bonaventure sees the significance of Christ crucified as the one who can truly restore us in the image of God. The cross is not an instrument used to vindicate sinful acts of violence and oppression. Rather, the cross is the expression of God's love for each of us. God has entered into suffering humanity, into the suffering corners of our lives, and has loved us precisely in and through this suffering. Undoubtedly, the cross belies human reason and we fail to grasp its meaning. In light of Bonaventure's thought, we might say that the cross is a failure unless the human heart can open up to it as the revelation of the compassionate love of God. In one of his meditations Bonaventure writes:

O my God, good Jesus,
Although I am in every way without merit and unworthy,
Grant to me, who did not merit to be present
At these events in the body, that I may ponder them
Faithfully in my mind and experience toward you,
My God crucified and put to death for me,
That feeling of *compassion.*[19]

What Bonaventure deeply and powerfully illustrates is that the cross is the axis of transformation—from the human heart of stone into a natural heart of love. The cross is a mandala[20] that integrates human weakness and divine compassion. Even more poignant in Bonaventure's writings is his emphasis that the cross of Jesus Christ is *our* life, *our* suffering, *our* image, the human image that is at once shackled by the pain of sin and capable of total self-giving love. Jesus Christ crucified is the truly human person, and the cross signifies the very paradox of humanity, vitiated by the desire for equality and power, yet, noble in the self-offering of life for another. As the Word of God, Christ is our openness to God and our hope that the image in which we are created *can* be realized in God.

For Bonaventure, to imitate Christ and to be restored in the image of God is ultimately a matter of compassionate love. It is becoming totally turned to God, radically dependent on God, and loving like God. It is Christ who shows us the way, who teaches us the truth about ourselves and about God, and who is the life of God in its fullest expression. The imitation of

Christ must ultimately break down the walls of the hardened heart and open one up to the truth of God's poor and humble self-giving love. Writing to a Poor Clare nun on how to progress in the spiritual life, Bonaventure states:

> Your heart is the altar of God. It is here that the fire of intense love must burn always. You are to feed it every day with the wood of the cross of Christ and the commemoration of his passion . . . . Let your love lead your steps to Jesus wounded, to Jesus crowned with thorns . . . there transformed into Christ by your burning love for the Crucified . . . transfixed by the sword of intimate compassion, seek nothing, desire nothing, wish for no consolation other than to be able to die with Christ on the cross. Then you may cry out with the Apostle Paul: With Christ, I am nailed to the cross. It is now no longer I that live, but Christ lives in me.[21]

Bonaventure's advice here is radical. Who of us can live each day hoping to die with Jesus on the cross? Who desires to be "transfixed" to the cross? In our contemporary culture, which can be appropriately described as "analgesic," we make every effort to avoid pain and suffering—whether physical, psychological or emotional. Not that we should advocate pain and suffering, no less seek it out. The question is, how do we live life in the most fulfilling way in the midst of a suffering world? How do we, who are created for happiness and peace, live immersed in a world shot through with sin? Bonaventure's answer is that the God of compassionate love, who has loved us precisely in and through our suffering humanity, offers us an example on the cross, an example of poverty and humility that enables us to turn totally to God and to live in compassionate love. The imitation of Christ, especially Christ crucified, is not about embracing pain and suffering; it is about where the center of our lives is located, how receptive we are to God's love and, in turn, how we share love with others. The example of Christ crucified shows that we are not to cling to anything but God and thus to place our absolute trust in God alone. The last word, as Bonaventure indicates, is not the cross of suffering but the victory of love which the suffering and death of Jesus Christ wins for us.[22]

Relationship to God who is, by nature, self-giving love allows Bonaventure to describe the restoration of the human image in Christ as a restoration in compassionate love. The cross is the axis of transformation because it is here that humility, poverty and love coinhere in such a way that they form the matrix of reconciliation and new life. God is love and only the poor and humble can share in the humble love of God.[23] The model Christian who Bonaventure holds up in his writings is Francis of Assisi. The crucified Christ penetrated the heart of Francis to such an extent that poverty and humility became the means of uniting himself with Christ on the cross. Bonaventure writes: "In all things / he wished / to be conformed to Christ crucified, / who hung on the cross poor, suffering, and naked."[24] By turning to God through the Crucified, Francis came to appreciate his absolute dependence on God. He began to recognize the truth of himself, his own unworthiness before God, and his "nothingness" apart from God. By facing God in humility and radical dependency, Francis became ever the more conformed to Christ crucified. He became restored in the image of the crucified God who is humble, self-giving love. Bonaventure interprets the Stigmata as the signs of Francis perfectly transformed in the image of Christ. In his *Major Legend of Saint Francis* he writes:

> After true love of Christ
> *transformed* the lover *into His image,*
> when the forty days were over . . .
> the angelic man Francis
> *came down from the mountain,*
> bearing with him
> the likeness of the Crucified,
> depicted not on *tablets of stone* or on panels of wood

carved by hand,
but engraved on parts of his flesh.[25]

Francis attained such inner conformity to Christ that he looked like Christ crucified in the flesh. It is the same type of conformity that Paul speaks about in his letter to the Galatians (2:20) when he writes: "I have been crucified with Christ, and the life I live now is not my own; Christ is living in me." Perhaps this idea of being crucified with the Crucified may deter some of us from pursuing this path but Paul goes on to say, "I still live my human life, but it is a life of faith in the Son of God, who loved me and gave himself for me." I think this sentence is key to what Bonaventure is saying and how he sees transformation in Christ, especially in light of Francis. To be conformed to Christ crucified and to be restored in the image of Christ is not to lose one's identity or uniqueness nor is it to be absorbed into Christ in some type of self-annihilation. Rather, it is the mystery of union, and is best stated in the terms of Pierre Teilhard de Chardin: union differentiates.[26] The more we are open to Christ and, in a particular way, to Christ crucified in our lives, the more we are open to the source of grace by which we follow the example and teaching of Christ. In turn, this leads us closer to God and to the truth of our lives in God. The more we are in union with Christ, the more truthful we become as human persons. When Francis descended the mountain as an icon of the Crucified, he did not descend *as* the Crucified: he descended as Francis, that is, as the truly loving person he was created to be. We can never *become* Jesus Christ (in the literal sense). The best that we can become is who God created us to be in our "unsinful selves," and that is only discovered in Christ who is Word and exemplar, and in whom the truth of all created reality resides. To be restored in the image of Christ is to become truly poor and humble, not to win other people's admiration or sympathy, but to become truthful in love. Christ lives in us when we live truthfully in Christ.

The question of whether or not we are to be restored in the image of God is ultimately a question of freedom. Francis *chose* to follow the poor and humble Christ, and Bonaventure emphasizes this freedom of choice in light of Francis. Commenting on the Stigmata of Francis, for example, Bonaventure writes: "St. Francis *chose* the highest poverty. It is fitting, therefore, that the sign of the Son of man, namely, Christ's cross, should be found on Saint Francis."[27] In light of Francis, Bonaventure indicates that if we recognize our human desire for God, which is integral to our being image of God, then we must also recognize that this desire is realized only in freedom. The desire for God is planted in the heart by grace but nurtured by prayers, tears, fasting and devotion. Once we recognize this desire we must then ask, do we choose poverty and humility as they intertwine in the inscrutable mystery of the cross, or do we choose the false poverty of a secular and materialistic world? Are we able to let go for the sake of the other, or do we cling to the other for the sake of self?

For Bonaventure, how we choose and what we choose makes a difference—first, in what we become by our choices, and second, what the world becomes because of our choices. The choice of following the poor and humble Christ cannot be a psychological one alone. Imitation by its very nature means expression, and the one who imitates Christ crucified in poverty and humility must express this relationship in a spirit of compassionate love.[28] In other words, to be restored in the poverty and humility of Christ crucified and to come to the truthfulness of our own humanity in God, one must be open to the cross—an openness that underscores the transformation of our lives both interiorly and exteriorly, the spirit in which we live and the flesh in which we act. Living in the spirit of Christ crucified, therefore, imparts new meaning to the cross. For the cross is not a means of vindicating wrongful action of violence and oppression. The cross is not something we give to others. Rather, the cross *is* what our lives become, that is, the shape they take in relation to our neighbors and to the created world around us.

To be formed in the image of Christ crucified is to live in the fundamental attitude of compassionate love. Bonaventure describes the perfection of love as being willing to suffer or die for one's neighbor. He writes: "As soon as we acquire charity, all that pertains to perfection becomes easy: acting or suffering, living or dying."[29] He sees the perfection of love expressed in the desire for martyrdom. It is this *spirit* of self-giving love, he indicates, that leads to peace for only when each of our lives takes the form of the cross will the cross of the world be lifted up in glory.[30]

The imitation of Christ, as it is sketched out in the writings of Bonaventure, is far more than literal mimicry—it is a theology of discipleship. It is that relationship with Christ that leads one to acknowledge one's poverty and humility before God and, thus, to acknowledge the truth of oneself in God. To imitate is to be restored as "image" which means, ultimately, to love like God, that is, by way of self-gift. It is to love God in a total way, to love others as ourselves, and to love all of creation with the spirit of compassion. For this reason, imitation of the poverty and humility of the Crucified is not simply a choice on the journey; rather, it is the heart of the spiritual journey and lies at the basis of a healing relation to the world.[31] It is the personal response to the deepest truth of one's being—that we are not of ourselves but we are of and for Another. It is to be expressive of whom we claim to be when we call ourselves "Christians."

Reflections

1. Pray using the gospel accounts of the crucifixion. How do these accounts speak to us about the poverty of God and the extent of God's love for us?

2. Where is poverty in my life? How do I view poverty and humility in relation to the imitation of Christ?

3. Pray using Luke 1:46–55. What does Mary's song tell us about our poverty in relation to God? How does Christ, especially Christ crucified, live out this prayer?

4. Pray using either Matthew 10:39, 12:22, or 16:24–27. Do I live with the desire for martyrdom, that is, in the spirit of compassionate love?

5. Who are my role models? How do I imitate the self-giving love of God?

Notes

1. This is an important question; however, without a theological foundation, it can lead to an unhealthy literalism that preempts the deeper meaning of following Christ. Imitation provides such a theological basis of discipleship, provided that it, too, does not fall prey to a fundamental literalism. Ambrose Nguyen Van Si examines the meaning of imitation in Bonaventure's theology, highlighting the distinction between imitating Christ and following Christ in the Franciscan tradition. See Ambrose Nguyen Van Si, "The Theology of the Imitation of Christ According to St. Bonaventure," *Greyfriars Review* 11 (Supplement, 1997): 1–181. See especially 29–35.

2. In his first book of the *Sentences*, Bonaventure states that where there is image there is imitation. Because only one substance can exist in God, the image which expresses him must be of the highest expression, implying the uniqueness of this total expression. See I *Sent.* d. 31, p. 2, q. 1, fund. 4 (I, 540a); I *Sent.* d. 31, p. 2, q. 2, concl. (I, 542a).

3. Peter Casarella, "The Expression and Form of the Word: Trinitarian Hermeneutics and the Sacramentality of Language in Hans Urs von Balthasar's Theology," *Renascence* 48.2 (Winter, 1996): 114–15. Casarella states, "form poured into appearances constitutes as well as conveys meaning. Form is the emergence of a concrete expression which co-determines the expressed content."

4. For Bonaventure, the imitation of Christ is grounded in exemplarism because the Word proceeds from the Father by reason of exemplarity. As the uncreated Word, the Son is the eternal exemplar of the Father. See Bonaventure, *Apologia pauperum* (hereafter *Apol. paup.*) 2.12 (VIII, 242b–243a); I *Sent.* d. 6, a.u., q. 3 (I, 129a–130b); Hayes, *Hidden Center*, 130–35.

5. *Apol. paup.* 2.13 (VIII, 243b); Hayes, *Center*, 123–37.

6. See *Perf. ev.* q. 1 (V, 121): Lig. *vit.* 5 (VIII, 72).
7. Delio, "Bonaventure's Metaphysics of the Good," 237.
8. Walter Kasper, *The God of Jesus Christ*, trans. Matthew O'Connell (New York: Crossroad, 1999), 195.
9. Zachary Hayes, commentary on "Sermon II on the Nativity," in *What Manner of Man*, 81, n.16.
10. *Hex.* 8.5 (V, 370a).
11. See *Lig vit.* 5–6 (VIII, 72).
12. *Sermon II on the Nativity* (IX, 106). Bonaventure begins his sermon by calling to mind the humility of God.
13. *Perf. ev.* q. 1 (V, 117–124).
14. Bonaventure viewed Francis as the paradigm of humility. In his evening sermon on Francis he states, "Saint Francis possessed this humility supremely. He loved and sought it, from the origin of his religious life until his death." Bonaventure goes on to describe the fruits of humility: 1) humility calms the anger of God, while moving him to suspend judgment due to guilt; 2) humility finds grace; 3) humility brings righteousness to perfection; 4) humility leads to eternal glory. See "The Evening Sermon on Saint Francis, 1255." Engl. trans. FA:ED II, 519.
15. *Hex.* 4.8 (V, 350); *Hex.* 10.17 (V, 379); II *Sent.* d. 1, p. 1, a. 3, q. 2, ad resp. (II, 34–35). For Bonaventure, humanity is ontologically rooted in poverty because humans are created by God and are essentially dependent on God.
16. III *Sent.* d. 1, a. 2, q. 3, ad resp. (III, 29–20); Hellmann, "Poverty: Franciscan Way to God," 341.
17. Hayes, *Hidden Center*, 142. Zachary Hayes offers profound insight on poverty and humility in Bonaventure's thought when he writes: "It is not an arbitrary, divine whim that the Son should become incarnate in the form of humility and poverty. His human nature and its history are the historical embodiment of his eternal Sonship. It must, therefore, reflect that eternal reality. It must reflect the truth of human reality as well, for this is grounded in the eternal Sonship. In the humility and poverty of the incarnate Word is the historical manifestation of the Son who is pure receptiveness of being and the full loving response to the Father. Thus, the incarnation in its concrete form reveals the authentic, ontological truth of the human situation." What Hayes identifies is the mutual coinherence between poverty, humility, and love of God. For Bonaventure, a true loving relationship with God must be grounded in poverty and humility. This is the only path of return to God.
18. Hayes, commentary on "Sermon II on the Nativity," in *What Manner of Man*, 89–90, n. 41.
19. *Lig. vit.* 32 (VIII, 80). Engl. trans. Cousins, *Bonaventure*, 158.
20. The term *mandala* is a Sanskrit word which is translated as "circle" or "center" or "that which surrounds." It is used primarily in eastern religions as an aid to contemplation. By meditating on the mandala symbol

or by participating in mandala ritual, one seeks to effect an inner transformation and to advance toward the goal of the spiritual journey. See Ewert Cousins, "Mandala Symbolism in the Theology of Bonaventure," *Cord* 21 (1971): 324–39.

21. *Perf. vit* 6.2 (VIII, 120). Engl. trans. De Vinck, "On the Perfection of Life," 239–40.

22. *Lig. vit.* 38 (VIII, 82).

23. See Hayes, *Hidden Center*, 143.

24. *Leg. maj.* 14.4 (EM, 117). Engl. trans. FA:ED II, 642.

25. *Leg. maj.* 13.5 (EM, 109). Engl. trans. FA:ED II, 634.

26. Pierre Teilhard de Chardin, *The Phenomenon of Man*, trans. Bernard Wall (New York: Harper & Row, 1959), 262. Teilhard de Chardin claims that "in any domain—whether it be the cells of a body, the members of a society or the elements of a spiritual synthesis—union differentiates. . . . The more 'other' they become in conjunction, the more they find themselves as 'self.' "

27. Bonaventure "The Evening Sermon on Saint Francis, 1262." Engl. trans. FA:ED II, 722.

28. See Ilia Delio, *Crucified Love*, 40–42.

29. Bonaventure *De triplici via* (hereafter *Tripl. via*) 2.12 (VIII, 10). Engl. trans. José de Vinck, "The Triple Way, or Love Enkindled," in *Mystical Opuscula*, vol. 1, *Works of Bonaventure* (Paterson, NJ: St. Anthony Guild Press, 1960), 78); Johann Baptist Metz, "In the Pluralism of Religious and Cultural Worlds: Notes Toward a Theological and Political Paradigm," trans. John Downey and Heiko Wiggers, *Cross Currents* (Summer, 1999): 227–36. Writing in view of political theology Metz asks, "might the authority of those who suffer bring diverse religious and cultural worlds together?" It is a question that, I believe, is answered in Bonaventure's theology of the crucified Christ.

30. *Tripl. Via* 3.11 (VIII, 17). Bonaventure links together the perfection of love, the desire for martyrdom and the attainment of peace. Peace is the fruit of compassionate love and is associated with the *desire* for martyrdom because this is the perfect love of Christ in imitation of his passion.

31. See Hayes, *Hidden Center*, 39.

Contemplation

One of the most attractive aspects of the spiritual journey is that progress in this path ultimately leads to contemplation. Some of us may think that contemplation is intended only for saints and mystics, others may see it as an unattainable goal. However, contemplation is that resting in God whereby one's entire life is centered in God and, we might say, God is the center of one's life. It is that mutual exchange in love, a sharing of the wills, as Bernard of Clairvaux described it, the nuptial union of the divine and human will. It is the ultimate transformation of one's life in God in which the heart beats with compassion and rests in the One it most desires. For Bonaventure, contemplation is the goal of Christian life.

The ancient Greeks described contemplation as a flight from the world, to gaze upon the "Mind" or ground of true reality.[1] For the Greeks, the material world including the body, held no real spiritual value and, thus, the spiritual path to ultimate truth necessitated that one transcend the world and subjugate the body to the spirit.[2] Bonaventure's understanding of contemplation is quite different from Greek thought and is radically Christocentric. As we said before, imitation for Bonaventure is to lead to contemplation.[3] In Bonaventure's view, contemplation cannot be exclusively confined to the soul since the soul itself cannot exist apart from the body. Rather, the Word of God entered into union with the flesh to ennoble our nature by creating the object of contemplation necessary for the beatification of our nature.[4] This object of contemplation for Bonaventure is not the transcendent unknowable God (as it was for the Greeks) but Christ, God and man. It is precisely in the humanity of Christ that God has enabled us to contemplate him: "And in my flesh I shall see God" (Jb 19:26).[5]

The humanity of Christ is essential to the contemplation of God because it is in the flesh that God is revealed. Christ became human to beatify the whole human and not just the soul alone.[6] Thus, Bonaventure indicates, Christ is teacher because he took on flesh and stood in our midst.[7] Divine wisdom, he states, which orders all things came in the flesh when she saw that order in the world had been corrupted. Christ, therefore, is the true light of knowledge who teaches interiorly and exteriorly. He teaches interiorly by way of the intellect and exteriorly by way of example, that is, as image and archetype. In light of the mystery of Christ, Bonventure describes contemplation as a twofold movement, a going-in to the divinity through the uncreated Word and a going-out to humanity through the incarnate Word.[8] To "go-in" to Christ is to enter into the mystery of Christ as the uncreated Word. To "go-out" to Christ is to imitate or follow the example of Christ as word and deed. We might find this idea difficult to grasp but it is essentially the experience of the mystics. Angela of Foligno confessed that as she prayed and meditated more deeply on the sufferings of Christ, she entered into the mystery of Christ as the uncreated Word.[9] So too, Bonaventure indicates that the more one enters into union with the one who is divine and human, Jesus Christ, the closer one comes to the contemplation of God.

If we understand contemplation as a twofold movement, we can say that in Bonaventure's thought, there really is no "going-in" to Christ without "going-out." One cannot be restored by the grace of Christ interiorly without expressing transformation through grace exteriorly. As Bonaventure describes it, contemplation is really an ascent and descent to God, and that is why it is linked to imitation.[10] The higher the soul ascends to God through divine illumination, the lower it descends in imitation of Christ. As the soul becomes "hierarchical" and, thus, illumined and perfected in Christ,[11] the body becomes shaped to the poverty, humility and suffering of Christ. Both soul and body, therefore, ascend and descend in conformity to Christ. This notion of contemplation as ascending and descending, interior and exterior, helps explain why saints such as Francis or Angela of Foligno could be attracted to the suffering of Christ and desire to imitate the passion of Christ. Attracted by God's love expressed through the suffering Christ, and interiorly transformed by grace, they entered into the mystery of the Word as eternal and incarnate. Striving for union with the Word, they became like the Word incarnate in spirit and flesh.

For Bonaventure, Francis is the perfect imitator of Christ. In one of his sermons he states that "he was made utterly Christ-like and configured to him" and because of this he reached the height of contemplation.[12] Francis "ascended in Christ" by entering more deeply into the mystery of God and descended in poverty and humility through imitation of the suffering humanity of Christ. In this way his life was grafted onto the "Tree of Life" which consists in "the vision, possession and enjoyment of God."[13] Bonaventure describes Francis's path to the contemplation of God according to a passage from the Song of Solomon:

> The Lord said to him: *Go up* because of me whom you shall contemplate at last and in that you will be glorified. We read in the Song of Solomon: *I will climb the palm tree and lay hold of its branches.* The palm tree has a trunk whose lower part is very narrow. The section nearest the ground is thinner than the higher section of the trunk which is not the case with any other tree. The palm tree is a figure of Jesus Christ, who in his humanity was made *a little less than the angels*, and was small and weak in this world, and in his divinity is Lord and Creator of the angels and of all things.[14]

If this path of ascending and descending in union with Christ is the path to contemplation, Bonaventure explores the ascending or interior path in a profoundly mystical way in his *Soul's Journey Into God*. Keeping in mind that this journey in union with Christ is a dynamic one, Bonaventure indicates that the interior movement is a continuous deepening within whereby one moves ever more deeply to the center of the soul and, thus, into the image in which the soul is formed. What this means, according to Bonaventure, is that relationship with Christ impels one to come closer to God interiorly, and in this coming closer, to gaze upon God in the fullness of the divine mystery.

In the *Soul's Journey* Bonaventure identifies the names of God as Being and Good. God is certainly Being because he is that Being than which no greater can be thought (Anselm's "Ontological Argument for the Existence of God"). God revealed himself as Being to Moses when he declared his name: "I Am who Am" (Ex 3:14). However, in the New Testament God reveals Godself as Good because Jesus says, "No one is good but God alone" (Lk 18:19; Mk 10:18). The name of God as Good in the New Testament allows Bonaventure to draw out the implications of this name for the mystery of Christ in the fullness of his divinity. Having already described the Trinity of persons according to the self-diffusive good in his commentary on the *Sentences*, he now returns to the Trinity and explores the properties of the divine persons based on the good. For the highest good to be self-diffusive, he writes, "it must be actual and intrinsic, substantial and hypostatic, natural and voluntary, free and necessary."[15] This immensity of divine goodness requires a beloved and a cobeloved, the one generated and the other spirated, and this is the Father and the Son and the Holy Spirit. "Unless these were present, it would by no means be the highest good because it would not diffuse itself in the highest degree."[16] In a most astounding and mystical way, Bonaventure explores the mystery of the divine persons distinguished by the good and realizes that, because of their properties, the Trinity is a coincidence of opposites. The Trinity is "eternal and present, simple and greatest, actual and unchangeable, perfect and immense, supremely one and all-inclusive"[17] as well as "supremely communicable with individuality of persons, supremely consubstantial with a plurality of hypostases, supremely coeternal with emanation, supremely mutually intimate with mission."[18] Knowledge of this "highest wonder" enables the mind to ascend to contemplation. With stunning mystical insight Bonaventure not only realizes that the Trinity is a coincidence of opposites but that Christ is a coincidence of opposites precisely because of the Trinity. In fact, the mystery of the Trinity of opposites *is* embodied in the mystery of Christ. As Bonaventure writes:

> If you are amazed because the divine Being is both first and last, eternal and most present, utterly simply and the greatest or boundless, totally present everywhere and nowhere contained, most actual and never moved . . . supremely one and yet all inclusive, containing all things in himself, being all power, all truth, all goodness—if you are this Cherub, look at the Mercy Seat [Christ crucified] and wonder that in him there is joined the first principle with the last, God with man, who was formed on the sixth day; the eternal is joined with temporal man, born of the Virgin in the fullness of time, the most simple with the most composite, the most actual with the one who suffered supremely and died, the most perfect and immense with the lowly, the supreme and all inclusive one with a composite individual distinct from others, that is, the man Jesus Christ.[19]

The mystery that penetrated Bonaventure's mind as he pondered the journey to God, is the mystery of Jesus Christ. He realized that Christ is not merely human nor the divine appearing in human form. Rather, Christ is truly divine and human and, as divine, embodies the entire Trinity in the mystery of his person. To enter into union with Christ, the truly human Christ, *is* to enter into the mystery of the Trinity. For Bonaventure, this can only take place in the context of the journey to God. As one moves interiorly into the center of one's soul, one "sees" the image to which one is made, namely, the Trinity which is recognized by the ability one has to know and love God. But the deeper one goes into the soul, the more it realizes that this image of the Trinity is focused in an exemplary way in Christ. Christ is the exemplary Image, therefore who fills the potential of the human person so that "when our mind contemplates Christ the Son of God, who is the image of the invisible God by nature, our humanity . . . reaches something perfect."[20]

Bonaventure's thought may be difficult to understand, and he himself must have struggled to describe the mystery because his language is highly symbolic. However, what he realized is that Christ is not simply *divine* and human, as if a single [monistic] God joined together with a single individual nature. Rather, Christ is divine as *Trinity* which is united to a single human nature.[21] As Trinity, Christ is not only relational self-giving love, but Christ is a coincidence of opposites because it is precisely as Word and center that the Trinity is focused in Christ.[22] In the Trinity, the Word is united to the Father and the Spirit and unites these persons in a common center. Similarly, in creation, the incarnate Word unites divinity and humanity in a common center. As the coincidence of opposites, Christ not only shares something of each opposite but the opposites are in union with each other precisely because they share a common ground in the Word who is center. As the incarnate Word, Christ is the center who unites body and soul which had become separated due to sin; as center of creation Christ unites human beings as neighbors, and human beings with non-human creation; as center between the Father and creation, Christ unites humanity and the universe itself with the Father. All of these unions are trinitarian unions of relationships: one is joined together with Christ through the Spirit who joins all together to the Father. Thus, Bonaventure indicates, if we come to this deepest understanding of the mystery of Christ deep within the soul, there will be nothing further to know. For we will not only come to the truth of God but we will come to the truth of our humanity as well as creation itself in God.

Yet, it is not simply a matter of knowledge. The image of Christ crucified at the center of the soul which Bonaventure symbolizes by the mercy seat (cf. Ex 25:20), is not about perfect knowledge alone. Rather, it is about our "image and likeness" and the noble potency of this image in the created order. The image in which we are created is aptly expressed by Jesus Christ crucified who is the true image and likeness of God. Although the Crucified is an image of opposites—divinity and humanity, strength and weakness, joy and sorrow, glory and pain—the Crucified is the image of the human condition now brought into union with the triune God of infinite love. Not only is the Crucified an image of who God is for us but as *our* image, Christ crucified is the image of what we are capable of, that is, loving by way of perfect self-gift. This is the capacity that lies at the heart of the human order, to be restored in the likeness of God through love. The image of Christ crucified is the center of the soul, therefore, because only through the Crucified can one attain divine likeness and truly contemplate God.[23]

In Bonaventure's view, the person of desire who has entered into the mystery of love through the wounds of the Crucified is led by love into a union with God. It is a union of love that is beyond knowledge or words, that is, a union in darkness because it is a love of such intensity and degree that the sheer luminosity of it renders the inner eye blind to the things of the physical senses or of the intellect. It is seraphic or burning love, a love that Francis of Assisi attained in union with Christ, enkindled in the fire of his passion. Ecstatic contemplation of the glory of God in the cross transforms one into the compassionate crucified Christ. This was Francis's experience on the mountain of La Verna where he received the Stigmata. As Wayne Hellmann writes:

> The "burning love" is the "passion of Christ" in which the soul is transformed into the depths of compassionate love. Seraphic love is compassionate love. It is indeed compassionate love that Bonaventure develops

> to the fullest. For Bonaventure, Francis's mystical experience of ecstatic contemplation of the transcendent glory of God transforms him into the compassionate crucified Christ. Seraphic glory and the divine intimacy of mystical contemplation not only places one in the seraphic order of angels. It places one on the cross, crucified with Christ.[24]

What Bonaventure points out in the *Soul's Journey* is that seraphic love is enflamed in the deepest part of the soul in such a way that God is known not by way of the intellect but by way of the spiritual senses which are awakened by the fire of love. With the mind asleep and the senses awake, the heart totally surrenders to God by the sheer attractive force of divine love. Bonaventure describes the crucified Christ as "spouse" and the ecstatic union of love as a mystical marriage, the "marriage of the cross." In his *Soliloquy* he writes:

> Christ on the cross bows his head, waiting for you, that he may kiss you; he stretches out his arms, that he may embrace you; his hands are open that he may enrich you; his body is spread out, that he may give himself totally; his feet are nailed, that he may stay there; his side is open for you that he may let you enter there.[25]

Francis is one who was truly united to the crucified Christ and who passed over into God through ecstatic contemplation. This, in Bonaventure's view, is the meaning of the Stigmata—Francis's pass over (*transitus*) in Christ crucified, in ecstatic contemplation. To "pass over in ecstatic contemplation" through Christ crucified follows the logic of love, not the logic of the mind. Knowledge alone cannot bring us into the mystery of God. While knowledge can help us grow in the love of God, such knowledge must ultimately yield to love. Thus, to arrive at the level of ecstatic contemplation is "mystical and secret, and no one knows this secret unless one desires it, and no one desires it except the one who is inflamed within the marrow of one's being by the fire of the Holy Spirit."[26] It is a passing over in union with the spouse, Christ crucified, to the mystery of the dynamic love of the Trinity. It is a transcendence of the mind whereby grace, desire, prayer, darkness and fire inflame the soul and carry one into God "by ecstatic unctions and burning affections." Bonaventure writes: "And this fire is God and Christ enkindles it in the heat of his burning passion."[27] Only in union with Christ crucified, Bonaventure indicates, a union joined by the flame of the Spirit's love, does one pass over into the Father of infinite love.[28]

Contemplation, in its mystical meaning, is a transcendent union in love. Bonaventure arrives at this insight because he realizes that God is not only Being but the triune God is the highest Good, that is, love. The human response, therefore, cannot simply be one of intellectual contemplation but must lead one into a union of love with the primordial mystery of love, that is, to be led back to a loving relationship between the Father and Son.[29] The passing over into God that Bonaventure describes at the end of the journey is an *ecstatic* (literally, "standing outside") contemplation because it is a total re-centering of oneself in God. It is, in Bonaventure's terms, a "mystical death" as he writes, "whoever loves this death sees God." It is a "death" because there is nothing in the intellect or in the physical senses that knows God. Rather, the mind stands in the heart and the heart is centered in God. At this stage of the journey, the spiritual senses alone now touch and taste the presence of God who is known only by the penetrating vision of love. One is drawn beyond oneself into the hidden mystery of the God of love who, as Crucified, embraces the inner soul with the wounds of love. It is a dying into love as Bonaventure writes: "Let us die then and enter into mystical darkness . . . with Christ crucified let us pass out of this world to the Father."[30] Christ crucified, therefore, is not only our example in love but leads us in love to the Father so that we can say: "It is enough."[31] One who arrives at this stage of the journey has only to surrender, like the Crucified, in total love to the Father so that through death one may pass over into the dominance of grace.[32] Although this final stage of union with the Crucified that leads to ecstatic contemplation seems radical, Bonaventure holds it up as the path for all Christians. It is not a special path for Franciscans or lofty mystics; rather, every spiritual person is to be, like Francis, wrapped in the poverty of the cross, contemplating the transcendent glory of God.[33] Every Christian, therefore, should desire ecstatic union with God and this means to desire that one's life be completely centered on the beloved and spouse, Christ crucified, in whom the Father of divine love is hidden.

It may be impossible to some and ridiculous to others that anyone should strive to be crucified with the Crucified in a desire to center one's life in God; yet, Bonaventure claims, this is the path to true wisdom. The goal of the spiritual journey is not only ecstatic contemplation, it is ecstatic wisdom. Christ crucified is the hidden treasure of wisdom and knowledge, and to be united to the Crucified is to partake of the divine wisdom.[34] In his commentary on the *Sentences,* Bonaventure describes wisdom as the experiential knowledge of God deepened by love.[35] It is wisdom that enables one to taste or delight in the divine as the fullness of love within the soul. Because wisdom is "knowledge in love" it imparts insight, a sense of the truth of things, and a deep awareness of God in the order of creation. It is wisdom that enables one to see with transforming vision the truth of all reality. Christ is the "book of wisdom" and one who knows Christ knows wisdom as the fount of creation and the light that permeates the beauty of creation.[36]

In describing the significance of Francis's Stigmata, Bonaventure writes that the Stigmata are "proof of Christian wisdom ploughed into the dust of your [Francis's] flesh."[37] Francis is the true Christian, the model and example for all to follow, because through union with the crucified Christ, his life was re-centered in God. With the eyes of wisdom and the heart of the Crucified, Francis saw the heart of reality with a penetrating gaze. Rather than being otherworldly or cut off from the world, Franciscan contemplation, as Bonaventure describes it, turns one toward the world. With the inner eye of love, one now reads the book of creation as the wisdom of God and one sees one's neighbor as the revelation of God. As Michael Blastic states, "Franciscan contemplation is horizontally ecstatic. That is, it takes one out of oneself and into the other; contemplation de-centers, making one receptive to the revelation of the truth of the other . . . as the effect of vision."[38]

To be restored in the contemplation of God is to be healed of the blindness that darkens the inner eye of the soul. The contemporary writer, Annie Dillard, tells the story of a blind girl who, blind from birth, is operated on by a brilliant surgeon. When the patches are removed several weeks later, the girl is not only able to see but she is stunned by the beauty of what she sees.[39] The story is a metaphor for our relationship to Christ who not only heals us of our blindness but restores in us the inner eye of love. This eye is the image of God illumined by wisdom and shaped by the love of the crucified Christ. To freely respond in love to divine love is to be receptive to the gift of grace that ultimately transforms the blindness of the inner eye into the dazzling light of authentic vision. By entering into the mystery of the Word within, the contemplative sees oneself and the whole of creation as the book of wisdom revealed in Jesus Christ. One "sees" rightly because one is no longer "bent over" by sin; knowledge in union with love impels the lover of God to stand upright before God without any demands. In the poverty of the cross and the fullness of divine love, the ecstatic contemplative is renewed in the innocence and freedom of paradise. Gazing upon the beauty of creation, one is drawn upward to God, outward to neighbor, and in descending solidarity with all of creation.[40] In union with Christ, therefore, one stands in a trinity of loving relationships. This is the goal of contemplation for Bonaventure, to participate in the Trinity of love, which is the fountain-fullness of happiness and peace.

Reflections

1. Pray or journal using the names of Christ as Spouse and Beauty. Is it easy for me to see beauty? Why or why not?

2. Pray over the text: "Christ on the cross bows his head, waiting for you, that he may kiss you; he stretches out his arms, that he may embrace you." How open am I to union with Christ crucified? How do I understand the relationship between suffering and love in my life?

3. How can I become more active in my contemplation and more contemplative in my action, thus, incarnating trinitarian love in the world?

4. Pray using Romans 12. How do I outwardly show what I believe? What hinders me?

5. Ask God to heal your love.

Notes

1. The word "contemplation" (*contemplatio*) is a Latin translation of the Greek *theoria* meaning, "looking at" or "gazing at." In the early church it connoted the idea of union with God, that is, gazing upon the face of God or resting in God. See Delio, *Crucified Love*, 174.

2. See, for example, Plato's "Allegory of the Cave" in which mortals, held bound by chains (of flesh) are unable to see the truth of reality which lies beyond, in the spiritual realm. See Bernard McGinn, *The Foundations of Mysticism: Origins to the Fifth Century*, vol. 1, *The Presence of God: A History of Western Christian Mysticism* (New York: Crossroad, 1994), 29; David Ross, *Plato's Theory of Ideas* (Oxford: Clarendon Press, 1951), 69.

3. In his *Breviloquium*, Bonaventure describes the role of the senses and imagination in leading one to contemplation. He writes: "It begins with speculation which starts from the senses, reaches the imagination, proceeds from the imagination to reason, from reason to the intellect, from the intellect to understanding, and from understanding to wisdom, that ecstatic knowledge which begins in this life and reaches fulfillment

in eternal glory." See *Brev*. 5.6 (V, 260). Engl. trans. De Vinck, *Breviloquium*, 206.

4. "Sermon II on the Nativity," in *What Manner of Man*, 67.

5. Ibid., 69.

6. "Christ, the One Teacher," in *What Manner of Man*, 33.

7. Bonaventure begins his sermon "Christ, the One Teacher of All" by stating: "Only one is your teacher, Christ." In his "Sermon II on the Third Sunday of Advent" he quotes from John (1:26): "In your midst is one you do not know." Since the notion of Christ as center or *medium* is integral to Bonaventure's thought, it is appropriate to say that Christ is the center, the one in our midst, who teaches us by word and example. See *What Manner of Man*, 21, 95.

8. "Christ, the One Teacher," in *What Manner of Man*, 31.

9. See, for example, the steps on Angela's progress in spiritual perfection in *Angela of Foligno*, 124–33.

10. In his sermon "Christ, the One Teacher," Bonaventure indicates that this going-in to the divinity and going-out to the humanity of Christ is, at the same time, the "ascent to heaven" and the "descent to earth" which is accomplished through Christ. See "Christ, the One Teacher," in *What Manner of Man*, 31; Delio, *Crucified Love*, 56.

11. *Hex*. 20.12, 22 (V, 327, 429). Bonaventure compares the hierarchization of the soul to the radiations of the Sun. Through the eternal Sun, that is, eternal wisdom, God lifts up the contemplative soul to the perception of eternal truth and reason. The hierarchized soul has a radiation that is constant, beautiful and joyful.

12. Bonaventure "Sermon on the Feast of the Transferal." Engl. trans. FA:ED II, 745.

13. FA:ED II, 746.

14. Ibid.

15. *Itin*. 6.2 (V, 310). Engl. trans. Cousins, *Bonaventure,* 103.

16. Ibid.

17. *Itin*. 5.7 (V,309).

18. *Itin*. 6.3 (V, 311). Engl. trans. Cousins, *Bonaventure,* 105.

19. *Itin*. 6.5 (V, 311). Engl. trans. Cousins, *Bonaventure*, 107.

20. *Itin*. 6.7 (V, 312). Engl. trans. Cousins, *Bonaventure*, 108–09.

21. Adriaan Peperzak, "Plotinian Motifs in Bonaventure's *Itinerary of the Mind to God*," in *Christian Spirituality and the Culture of Modernity*, ed. Peter Casarella and George P. Schner (Grand Rapids: William B. Eerdmans, 1998), 61–2. In an insightful essay on contemplation in Plotinus and Bonaventure, Peperzak explores the incomprehensible mystery that captures Bonaventure in the final stages of the journey to God. The mystery is rooted in the idea that God is self-diffusive goodness and, thus, self-communicative. "What Bonaventure finds really surprising, incomprehensible, and admirable," he states, "is not so much God's unicity and God's trinity taken separately, but rather their simultaneity and mutual inclusiveness. . . . The theological concentration on

God's being one *and* threefold in love is not the end stage of the journey, he indicates, rather the traveler is directed to the Mercy Seat [Christ Crucified] to admire something even more wonderful than the 'superadmirable union of God and humanity in the unity of Christ's person.' This is the center and synthesis in which the union of God's being and his trinity expresses itself as the perfect union of the Creator and his creation: Christ [Crucified] is the human icon in which the Word of the Origin has become the open book in which all essential truths can be found."

22. *Hex.* 9.2 (V, 373); *Hex.* 3.7 (V, 344); Zachary Hayes, "Christology and Metaphysics in the Thought of Bonaventure," *Journal of Religion* (Supplement, 1978): S91; Ibid., *Hidden Center*, 160.

23. *Itin.* prol. 3 (V, 295).

24. Wayne Hellmann, "The Seraph in the Legends of Thomas of Celano and St. Bonaventure: The Victorine Tradition," vol. 1, *Bonaventuriana: Miscellanea in onore di Jacques Guy Bougerol*, ed. Francisco de Asis Chavero Blanco (Rome: Edizione Antonianum, 1988), 355.

25. *Solil.* 1.39 (VIII, 41b). Engl. trans. De Vinck, "Soliloquy," 69.

26. *Itin.* 7.4 (V, 312). Engl. trans. Cousins, *Bonaventure,* 113.

27. *Itin.* 7.6 (V, 313). Engl. trans. Cousins, *Bonaventure,* 115.

28. *Itin.* 7.6 (V, 313). Bonaventure quotes from the Gospel of John (13:1) saying, "With Christ crucified let us pass out of this world to the Father so that when the Father is shown to us, we may say with Philip: It is enough for us." Engl. trans. Cousins, *Bonaventure*, 116.

29. Delio, *Crucified Love*, 75–6. While the goal of the spiritual journey is union with God, it is, at the same, perfection in love. One who arrives at the final stage of the journey becomes transcendent in love. In union with Christ crucified, God inter-penetrates one's being and imparts a dynamic and creative presence that opens one to infinite possibilities, to be creative and to transcend oneself. Bonaventure describes this perfection in love, which is really love in imitation of the Crucified, as a desire for martyrdom and peace. See *Tripl. via* 2.11 (VIII, 10–11).

30. *Itin.* 7.6 (V, 313).

31. Ibid. Cousins, *Bonaventure*, 116.

32. Peperzak ("Plotinian Motifs," 62) examines the final chapters of the "Soul's Journey" in light of union and states: "The theosis of human mortals is realized in God's mortality. Encountering God is not an escape from corporeality, but the acceptance of mortality as a symbol and concretization of absolute generosity and self-communication. . . . Death is necessary, not in order to free the soul from its imprisonment in corporeality, but rather to pass over into the dominance of grace."

33. In his sermons on Saint Francis, Bonaventure clearly indicates that the Stigmata are the signs that Francis attained the heights of contemplation. They are the imprint of Christ crucified on the heart of Francis whose ardent love of Christ forged him into his likeness. Thus, for Bonaventure, everyone who, like Francis, desires to attain this goal of

contemplation "will have to bear these signs." See "Sermon 2 on St. Francis," in *Disciple and Master*, 84, 93–4.

34. In his *Hexaëmeron* (1.11) Bonaventure states that in Christ are hidden all the treasures of wisdom and knowledge.

35. III *Sent.* d. 35, a. 1, q. 1, concl. (III, 774ab); Zachary Hayes, "Franciscan Tradition as a Wisdom Tradition," *Spirit and Life: A Journal of Contemporary Franciscanism* 7 (1997): 27–40.

36. *Brev.* 2.11 (V, 229); *Lig. vit.* 46 (VIII, 84).

37. *Leg. maj.* 13.10 (EM, 114). Engl. trans. FA:ED II, 639.

38. Michael Blastic, "Contemplation and Compassion: A Franciscan Ministerial Spirituality," *Spirit and Life: A Journal of Contemporary Franciscanism* 7 (1997): 168.

39. Annie Dillard, *Pilgrim at Tinker Creek* (New York: Harper's Magazine Press, 1974), 29. Dillard's insightful second chapter entitled "Seeing" provides stories of human life that complement Bonaventure's theology of contuition or seeing the truth of things in relation to God.

40. This is how Bonaventure views Francis, the exemplary Christ-mystic. See *Leg. maj.* 8.1 (VIII, 64).

Peace

We are all on a journey of some sort, and while most of us are aware of being on a spiritual journey, it is a question of how many of us consider the goal of our journey. That is, is the journey simply an open one with an unlimited horizon of possibilities? Or do we have in mind an ultimate goal that we are striving for? In his *Soul's Journey Into God*, Bonaventure clearly points out that the goal of the spiritual journey is ecstatic contemplation which, in his view, is peace.

Peace. The word itself brings harmony. It is a word that our contemporary world hungers for, kills for and dies for. It is a word that is meaningful for some and meaningless for others, especially for those living in parts of the world conditioned by violence and oppression. There is not a human person in the world who does not hunger for peace because the hunger for peace is the hunger for love, and every human person is created to love. Thus, humanity desires peace—inner peace, communal peace and historical peace. This is the goal, I believe, of the world's spiritual journey—peace—because all of humanity, in some way, hungers for God.

Bonaventure admits that he was seeking peace when he went up to the mountain of La Verna where he composed the *Soul's Journey*. On that mountain while meditating on the life of Francis and his conformity to the crucified Christ, Bonaventure realized that Francis was truly a man of peace because he arrived at the level of perfect love. In the prologue of the *Soul's Journey*, Bonaventure highlights Francis as the model and guide to that peace "which surpasses all understanding." He writes:

> At the beginning and end of every sermon
> he announced peace;

in every greeting he wished for peace;
in every contemplation he sighed for ecstatic peace—
like a citizen of that Jerusalem of which
that Man of Peace says,
who was peaceable with those who hated peace:
Pray for the peace of Jerusalem.[1]

In Bonaventure's view, Francis became a man of peace because he lived his life in the poverty of the desert, relying on the goodness of God alone. From the beginning of his conversion, peace marked the path of Francis's life. Describing Francis as a "leader and herald of gospel perfection," Bonaventure writes: "*The Most High God looked upon* him, / *a little, poor, and contrite man,* / . . . that . . . he might *prepare for the Lord a way* of light *and peace* / to the hearts of his faithful."[2] This way of peace, however, began in the heart of Francis himself, for he seemed to have desired peace with the same intensity that he desired God.

The desire for peace, according to Bonaventure, cannot be fulfilled apart from the desire for God; therefore, peace can be sought only within the context of the spiritual journey to God.[3] Peace is not an object to possess; rather, it is based on relationship to God. It can be gained only by receiving from another. It is receptivity that must be grounded in love. Peace flows out of the Trinity of love. It is a gift given by the Father to the Son and, in turn, given by Christ to his disciples to share with others so as to renew the Trinity of love in history. Just as Jesus had sent the seventy-two disciples out on mission to proclaim the good news of God's reign, so too Francis prepared his disciples to give the blessing of peace so that people's hearts could receive the central gospel message: God's loving reign.[4] Thomas of Celano states that Francis began his preaching ministry by emphasizing the importance of peace:

> In all his preaching, before he presented the word of God to the assembly, he prayed for peace saying, "May the Lord give you peace." He always proclaimed this to

> men and women, to those he met and to those who met him. Accordingly, many who hated peace along with salvation, with the Lord's help wholeheartedly embraced peace. They became themselves children of peace, now rivals for eternal salvation.[5]

The source of Francis's peace was Christ. Inwardly liberated from the ego's grasp of self-desires by the love of the Crucified, Francis attained an inner peace of mind. He came to live as if he had already entered the heavenly Jerusalem. Such peace, Bonaventure writes, arose out of the peaceful reconciliation within Francis's own being itself, that is, the reconciliation of his body and soul in union with God. In his *Major Legend of Saint Francis* Bonaventure writes: "[Francis] had reached such purity that his flesh was in remarkable harmony with his spirit and his spirit with God."[6] Because of Christ, peace became rooted in Francis's being, at the very heart of his life. It was a peace that took root in the very center of his soul and radiated outward to the community around him, ultimately bearing its effects on the shape of history itself.

The inner peace that Francis attained enabled him to be at peace with all of creation. "As a result," Bonaventure states, "God ordained / that creation which serves its Maker / should be subject in an extraordinary way / to his [Francis's] will and command."[7] Francis's inner peace, which flowed from his transformation in Christ's love, could not be contained simply within himself; rather, like an inner spring of self-diffusion it radiated to all of creation. We might say that Francis's inner eye, imbued with peace, recognized the justice of creation because in union with Christ he became conscious of the beauty and wisdom of creation as the marvelous work of God. As Bonaventure writes:

> In beautiful things
> He saw Beauty itself
> And through his vestiges imprinted on creation
> he followed his Beloved everywhere

making from all things a ladder
By which he could climb up
and embrace him who is utterly desirable.[8]

All things became, for Francis, a sign of God's overflowing goodness. Just as the divine goodness was fully revealed in Christ, Francis came to recognize Christ in all things. He developed a profound sense of "true piety," that is, a sense of being deeply related to each and every thing which he expressed in the form of compassionate love. It is piety, Bonaventure states, that restored him to the state of original innocence through universal reconciliation with each and every thing.[9] He showed tender compassion for all those suffering from affliction. "When he considered the primordial source of all things," Bonaventure writes, "he was filled with even more abundant piety, calling creatures no matter how small, by the name of brother or sister, because he knew they had the same primordial source as himself."[10] Francis showed compassionate love even to animals who were wild and dangerous. Bonaventure devotes a section of his biography to Francis and his relation to animals: how he admonished sheep, blessed a fish, brought a flock of birds to obedience and tamed the ferocious wolves at Greccio.[11] Francis's peace, which he shared with creation, not only flowed out of his loving relationship with Christ but he became, like Christ, a mediator in creation reconciling the various members of creation to one another and leading all to proper relationship in God. His *Canticle of the Creatures* is a hymn that expresses his deep sense of relationship with all the elements of creation. It is a hymn replete with the melody of love that unites all of creation in Christ, the center of peace. Although the rhythm of the *Canticle* flows like a river, the last sections were composed at different times. When Francis had learned of the "savage hatred" that had developed between the bishop of Assisi and the mayor, he was "pained to see that no one, religious or lay, intervened to establish peace and concord between them."[12] At the end of the *Canticle*, therefore, he added a strophe in praise of peace: "Praise be You, my Lord through those who give pardon for Your love, / and bear infirmity and tribulation. / Blessed are they who endure in peace, / for by You, Most High, they shall be crowned."[13] In Francis's view, true peacemakers are those willing to suffer for peace and endure all in peace for the sake of the Gospel.

Francis's peace emerged from his relationship with the *crucified* Christ. Peace was the fruit of his willingness to suffer in, with and for another—for Christ—and for all those redeemed by Christ. Francis's life became a life of peace as he became more deeply immersed in the mystery of the cross. His was not a piety or peace of "feeling good about himself"; rather, it was the peace of ecstatic union, of becoming re-centered in God through transformation in the crucified Christ. In his Admonition XV where he comments on the beatitude, "Blessed are the peacemakers for they shall be called the children of God" (Mt 5:9), Francis writes: "Those people are truly peacemakers who, regardless of what they suffer in this world, preserve peace of spirit and body out of love of our Lord Jesus Christ."[14] For Francis, it is better to suffer for peace than to triumph through violence.[15] Bonaventure describes the path to peace as the path to perfect love, the type of love that should express itself in the desire for martyrdom. Keenly aware of the gift of Christ's peace rooted in love, he wrote that peace is the perfection of love, a love which is enkindled through union with Christ crucified. It bears the marks of poverty and humility in imitation of the Crucified, being turned toward God as the source of every good gift and the neighbor as the reflection of God in creation. The peaceful person "sees rightly," that is, the truth of reality, with the vision of the inner eye of love.

Although the highest stage of love, ecstatic contemplation, is that perfect union with God, Bonaventure did not see contemplation excusing one from responsibility to the world. Conversely, he maintained that perfect love should impel one into the world. Bonaventure is dependent here on the thought of Richard of St. Victor. According to Richard, in the highest degree of love "the soul goes forth on God's behalf and descends below herself . . . because of her neighbor."[16] Suffering compassion and the humble descent below oneself manifest the perfection of love in God. In the *Triple Way*, Bonaventure explores the significance of compassionate love that leads to peace. Peace, he indicates, cannot be had without perfect charity; thus, one who attains perfect love attains peace. The six degrees of love that lead to perfect charity are: sensitivity, avidity, satiety, ebriety, security, and tranquility.[17] What Bonaventure means by these various degrees of love is that one progresses in love toward perfect love of God: from loving God for the sake of self-satisfaction to loving God for the sake of God alone. In the fourth degree, for example, the love of God is so great that "one is not only disgusted with consolation, but instead of it, loves and seeks the cross."[18] In the fifth degree, security, Bonaventure says, "the soul feels that it loves God so much that it would happily bear for its sake every punishment and every shame, fear is readily expelled, and the soul conceives such hope in the divine assistance that it believes no power could cut it away from God."[19] The movement toward perfect love, therefore, is a progression in loving the other for the sake of the other and not for any other reason. This is why Bonaventure sees Christ crucified as the model of perfect love and describes the attainment of perfect love as a progression through the cross. He writes: "In the first the world is crucified to the person; in the second the person is crucified to the world; in the third the person is crucified for the sake of the world."[20] By persevering through the six degrees of love one ascends in love to perfect peace because the perfection of love leads to perfection in all else—acting or suffering, living or dying—one is ready to give all out of love for God and neighbor.[21] "Here great peace is found," Bonaventure states, "the very consummation, as it were of the peace the Lord left with the Apostles."[22] This level of peace and perfect love is the desire for martyrdom. It is the desire to love one's neighbor by way of self-gift out of love for God. As Bonaventure writes:

> Only is perfection attained when one finds one's heart not merely willing, but intensely longing, to die for one's neighbor's salvation, according to the words of St. Paul: I will most gladly spend and be spent for your souls. We cannot love our neighbor perfectly before we attain a perfect love of God. It is for him that we love our neighbor: only because of him that we find our neighbor lovable.[23]

Bonaventure indicates that the highest level of love, peace, is the fruit of union with the Crucified. It is the state of inner tranquility, the willingness to follow Christ in the cross even to death, and the desire to offer one's life completely for the salvation of others in imitation of Christ. Bonaventure saw this expression of perfect love in the life of Francis, in his willingness to suffer martyrdom for the sake of the Gospel, and his willingness to embrace and heal the leper with the kiss of compassion. By the wounds of the Stigmata Francis became the herald of peace since, like Christ, he was willing to sacrifice all for love. After descending the mountain where he was marked by the signs of the cross in the flesh, he returned to his ministry among the lepers. This is how Bonaventure describes him:

> Now fixed with Christ to the cross, in both body and spirit, Francis not only burned with a Seraphic love of God but also thirsted with Christ crucified for the salvation of all people. . . . He was ablaze with a great desire to return to the humility he practiced at the beginning; to nurse the lepers as he did at the outset and to treat like a slave once more his body that was already in a state of collapse from his work.[24]

Bonaventure came to realize that the Stigmata of Francis not only had spiritual significance, that is, they not only symbolized his union with Christ but they marked him as an eschatological figure, one who had reached the final age of peace and whose example would lead all to peace at the end of time.[25] In a series of lectures on the *Six Days of Creation*, Bonaventure described the quest for peace by mapping out the journey of the world through Christ the center. As he envisioned it, this journey was one that was destined for peace whereby the Church militant would yield to the Church triumphant before the consummation of the world. What Bonaventure realized by the end of his life is that, as the soul must find its way back to God through Christ the center, so too the world follows a similar journey whereby it is to return to God through the burning love of the Crucified.[26] His vision of world peace was undoubtedly a culmination of years reflecting on the life of Francis, the meaning of the Stigmata and the fate of the Order [and the Church] in the face of so many divisions.

The emphasis that Bonaventure placed on peace in the context of the cross probably reflects his own search for peace throughout his life. It is likely that the contentions of the Joachites within the Franciscan Order impelled him to strive for peace at every level of life. Bonaventure's reaction to the thought of Joachim of Fiore is complex but he seemed to have been influenced by this Cistercian abbot with regard to the end of history.[27] Joachim envisioned history as a working out of the Trinity within history. He devised a series of patterns to describe the movement of history toward its culmination in the Trinity, not all of which were readily accepted. Bonaventure was influenced by one of his patterns of history, however, the *secunda diffinitio*, which divided history into two main periods, the Old Testament and the New Testament, each with seven periods joined by Christ at the center.[28] In the New Testament period of history, the period we are currently in, Joachim prophesied that spiritual people (contemplatives) would emerge within history and would mark the age of peace. Bonaventure indicated that Joachim's prophecy was fulfilled in the person of Francis. In a time when sin had grown stronger, faith and love had weakened, and the Church itself had become corrupt, Francis was sent by God to renew the evangelical life in a world that was crumbling in ruins and soon coming to an end.

Bonaventure saw Francis as the truly spiritual person, the one who was conformed to Christ and shaped in compassionate love. The Stigmata of Francis, by which he bore a likeness to the Crucified in his flesh, reflected his likeness to Christ crucified in his spirit. That Francis became a man of peace because of his likeness to Christ signified to Bonaventure that peace is not only realizable in history but can only be realized in union with Christ.[29] Francis's attainment of the final age of mystical peace indicates that this age of peace is to be both mystical and historical. It is the fruit of ecstatic union with Christ crucified. Bonaventure did not view Francis as a model of peace for Franciscans alone; rather, all spiritual women and men, mendicants and non-mendicants, who desire peace, must strive for union with Christ.

The implications of Bonaventure's ideas on the relationship between Francis and historical peace are radical. He saw within the Church a Seraphic Order of spiritual men and women whose burning love of Christ would be expressed outwardly in their willingness to suffer and die for their neighbors in a spirit of compassionate love. In his lectures at Paris, Bonaventure described this Order stating: "This Order [the Seraphic Order] will not flourish unless Christ appears and suffers in his mystical body."[30] In the final age, he indicated, "there will be a consummation of those sufferings of Christ which he now bears in his [mystical] body."[31] Bonaventure's language is somewhat obtuse and his meaning is difficult to grasp but the notion that Christ is to appear and suffer connotes a sign like that of Francis's Stigmata. In a sermon on Saint Francis he indicates that "everyone will have to bear this sign" [the Stigmata] as a sign of the mystical body of Christ, for as Saint Paul says: "those who belong to Christ Jesus have crucified the flesh with its passions and desires" (Gal 5:24)[32] The final age of peace, according to Bonaventure, will only come about when those who are conformed to Christ in the spirit will express this union in the flesh and in the willingness to suffer for others. This inward-outward expression *is* the mystical appearance of Christ in that Christ appears in his own image, that is, in each person who is united to him and restored in his love. Just as Francis appeared as an image of the Crucified by receiving the Stigmata, so too those, like Francis, must be inwardly inflamed by the fire of love and outwardly marked by the sign of the cross. Cruciform love and the desire for martyrdom mark the final age of peace. As Christ appeared in Francis through the wounds of his flesh, so too will Christ appear in the world through the wounded flesh of those who have made the journey in love to union with God.[33]

If Bonaventure saw that history can reach an age of peace before it comes to an end, he was also aware that such an age cannot be attained by force or domination. Peace, historical peace, is deeply rooted in love. The Seraphic Doctor maintained that the final age of peace is firmly rooted in the human person as image of God, and the human freedom to turn toward God in Christ. And because peace is possible in the human person, it is possible in history. The final age of peace, therefore, is grounded in Christian piety, in the humanity of Christ and in the willingness to love and suffer like Christ. Where there is Christ there is love and where there is love there is peace. Because of this, Christians have a responsibility for the world—not to avoid it or evade it but to embrace it in compassionate love. It is into the hands of Christians that the peace of the world has been entrusted and until those hands are marked by the wounds of the Crucified, peace will not be realized.

If we follow Bonaventure's thought through his labyrinth of symbolic language, we come to realize that peace is a choice. If we desire peace then we must choose Christ and him crucified, and if we choose Christ crucified we must be willing to suffer and die for the sake of the Gospel. The desire for martyrdom is a spirit of compassionate love but it is also a reality—a harsh reality for those of us who like comfort and want to avoid pain. But if comfort is our choice, then we must ask, what is the goal of our journey? For the capacity of the human person is the capacity of the world, and if our capacity for God is realized in Christ who reconciles all opposites within us, so too it is Christ who stands at the center of healing and wholeness in the world. There will be no peace [in the world], Bonaventure states, until Christ appears and suffers in his mystical body. Can Christ appear in the world apart from us who call ourselves "Christians?" Clearly, in Bonaventure's mind, peace must flow out of an inner source of love and be expressed in the actions of our lives. Thus, if we fail in love we fail in peace, and if we fail in peace we must bear the triumph of violence. Such is the sorrow of being called Christian or the joy of loving Christ.

Reflections

1. Do I view peace as the absence of conflict or as the fruit of my relationship with Christ? What am I willing to sacrifice or not sacrifice for the sake of peace?

2. Peace must be found in the present circumstances of our lives. Do I find peace even in the difficult events of life? Why or why not? How do I embrace the search for peace and the willingness to suffer in union with Christ?

3. Pray using John 14:1–4, 15–19, 25–27. In the light of the cross, Jesus imparts his peace to us. How do I accept the gift of Christ's peace and share it with others? What hinders me from being open or receptive to this gift of peace?

Notes

1. *Itin.* prol. 1 (V, 295). Engl. trans. Cousins, *Bonaventure*, 53–4.
2. *Leg. maj:* prol. (EM, 3). Engl. trans. FA:ED II, 525.
3. In the prologue to his "Soul's Journey," Bonaventure indicates that he went up to the mountain of La Verna in search of peace. "I was seeking this peace with panting spirit," he writes, and realized, "there is no other path than through the burning love of the Crucified." See Cousins, *Bonaventure,* 54.
4. Charles Finnegan, "Proclaim Peace to All," *Cord* 41 (1991): 270.

5. Thomas of Celano, *The Life of Saint Francis* 23. Engl. trans. FA:ED I, 203.

6. *Leg. maj.* 5.9 (EM, 45). Engl. trans. FA:ED II, 567.

7. Ibid.

8. *Leg. maj.* 9.1 (EM, 74). Engl. trans. FA:ED II, 596. This passage clearly shows Bonaventure's understanding of the exemplary world. Francis, in union with Christ, has that "contuitive" vision that sees the heart of reality. In light of Bonaventure's epistemology, one can say s/he knows each thing better in God than in his/her very self. See Cousins, *Coincidence of Opposites*, 118.

9. *Leg. maj.* 8.1 (EM, 64).

10. *Leg. maj.* 8.6 (EM, 68). Engl. trans. Ewert Cousins, *Bonaventure: The Soul's Journey Into God, The Tree of Life, The Life of St. Francis* (New York: Paulist, 1978), 254.

11. *Leg. maj.* 8, 6–10 (EM, 68–72). The notion that Francis returns to the state of original innocence in union with Christ the New Adam underscores the section on animal stories which Bonaventure recounts in the *Legenda maior*. From earliest times, Christian teaching has pointed to Christ as the new Adam who restores through obedience the paradise that the first Adam lost through disobedience (cf. Rom 5:12–21 on the two Adams). It is an anticipation of the messianic fulfillment at the end of the ages where there will be a new heaven and a new earth. See Jean Daniélou, *Sacramentum Futuri: Études sur les origines de la typologie biblique* (Paris: Vrin., 1950), 4–5.

12. *Legenda perugina* 44. Engl. trans. Finnegan, "Proclaim Peace," 268.

13. Francis of Assisi "The Canticle of the Creatures." Engl. trans. FA:ED I, 114.

14. Francis of Assisi "Admonition XV." Engl. trans. FA:ED I, 134.

15. Finnegan, "Proclaim Peace to All," 268.

16. Richard of St. Victor "The Four Degrees of Passionate Charity," in *Selected Writings on Contemplation*, trans. Clare Kirchberger (London: Faber and Faber, 1957), 224.

17. *Tripl via*. 2.9–11 (VIII, 10).

18. *Tripl. via*. 2.11 (VIII, 10). Engl trans. De Vinck, "Triple Way," 78.

19. Ibid.

20. *Tripl. via*. 2.8 (VIII, 9b). Engl. trans. De Vinck, "Triple Way," 76.

21. *Tripl. via*. 2.11 (VIII, 11). Engl. trans. De Vinck, "Triple Way," 79.

22. *Tripl. via*. 2.12 (VIII, 11). Engl. trans. De Vinck, "Triple Way," 79.

23. *Tripl. via*. 2.8 (VIII, 9–10). Engl. trans. De Vinck, "Triple Way," 76–7. E. R. Daniel has examined Bonaventure's desire for martyrdom in the context of the mystical ascent toward union with God and eschatological renewal. See Daniel, *Franciscan Concept of Mission,* 50–54; Ibid., "The Desire for Martyrdom: A Leitmotiv of St. Bonaventure," *Franciscan Studies* 30 (1972): 74–87.

24. *Leg. maj.* 14.1 (EM, 115). Engl. trans. Cousins, *Bonaventure,* 315.

25. The prologue of Bonaventure's "The Legend of Saint Francis" (*Leg. maj*) clearly shows that Bonaventure viewed Francis as an eschatological figure. He describes him as the "angel of true peace . . . ascending from the rising of the sun bearing the seal of the living God." See *Leg. maj.* prol. 1 (EM, 2). Engl. trans. FA:ED I, 526, 527.

26. See Ilia Delio, "From Prophecy to Mysticism: Bonaventure's Eschatology in Light of Joachim of Fiore," *Traditio* 52 (1997): 153–77.

27. Joachim of Fiore, also referred to as the "Calabrian abbot," was a Cistercian abbot of a monastery in Corazzo in the early 1180s. Around 1190, he left the Cistercian order and founded his own monastery at San Giovanni in Fiore in the alpine sila plateau of Calabria. For the details of his life, see Bernard McGinn, *The Calabrian Abbot: Joachim of Fiore in the History of Western Thought* (New York: Macmillan, 1985).

28. For a discussion on Joachim's patterns of history, see E. Randolph Daniel, "Joachim of Fiore: Patterns of History in the Apocalypse," in *Apocalypse in the Middle Ages,* ed. Richard K. Emmerson and Bernard McGinn (Ithaca: Cornell University Press, 1992), 72–88; cf. E. Randolph Daniel ("St. Bonaventure's Debt to Joachim," in *Medievalia et Humanistica*, ed. Paul Maurice Colgan [Totowa: Rowman and Littlefield, 1982], 61–74) who has shown that Bonaventure was influenced by Joachim's *secunda diffinitio.*

29. See Delio, "From Prophecy to Mysticism," 163–64.

30. *Hex.* 22. 23 (V, 441). Engl. trans. De Vinck, *Six Days of Creation*, 352.

31. *Hex.* 20.15 (V, 428). Engl. trans. De Vinck, *Six Days of Creation*, 309.

32. "The Evening Sermon on Saint Francis, 1262." Engl. trans. FA:ED II, 720.

33. Delio, "From Prophecy to Mysticism," 169–75.

Reductio

All things must lead back to God

In his first lecture on the *Six Days of Creation* given to the students at the University of Paris a year before his death,[1] Bonaventure arrived at the fullness of his vision. "This is our entire metaphysics," he exclaimed, "emanation, exemplarity, and consummation, that is, illumination through spiritual radiations and return to the Most High" through Christ the center.[2] As if putting together the pieces of a divine puzzle, Bonaventure realized that God, humanity and creation are united in Jesus Christ. And because Christ is the image and model for the human person, the divine plan of love poured out into the mystery of creation is brought to perfection by the human person. Bonaventure was a realist who formulated his theology with a clear historical consciousness. If he was aware that everything comes from God, he was equally aware that the dynamism of history undergirds the return of all things to God. And in light of this task, he saw the profound role of the human person upon whom the destiny of history depends.

Bonaventure used the term *reductio* to describe the leading back of all reality to its basic principle, namely, the triune God.[3] The exemplary world of creation which flows out of the goodness of God has meaning and purpose only in light of the human person who, created in the image of God, recognizes God in the signs of creation and, in turn, gives praise, reverence and thanks. "In the state of innocence at the beginning of human history," Bonaventure writes, "the human person had knowledge of created things and was led to God because of the image-reflectiveness of created things, and as a consequence, praised, honored and loved God. This is the reason for creation and in this way all creatures are led back to God."[4] What Bonaventure envisioned as original creation, therefore, was not only the bringing into existence of created reality but the central role of the human person in creation, one who could recognize the divine imprint in each and every thing and give praise and glory to God. Bonaventure's insight is reflected in the life of Francis of Assisi who by the end of his life had returned to God and who, in this return, recognized creation as the manifestation of God's glory. In his "Canticle of the Creatures" Francis sings the praises of God in solidarity with all the elements of creation:

> *Praised* be You, my Lord, through Brother *Wind*,
> and through the air, cloudy and serene, and every kind of weather
> through whom You give sustenance to Your creatures.
> *Praised* be You, my Lord, through Sister *Water*,
> who is very useful and humble and precious and chaste.
> *Praised* be You, my Lord, through Brother *Fire*,
> through whom *You light the night*
> and he is beautiful and playful and robust and strong.
> *Praised* be You, my Lord, through our Sister Mother *Earth*,
> who sustains and governs us,
> and who produces various fruit with colored flowers and *herbs*.[5]

The "Canticle" resounds with the loving voice of Francis, who expresses the unity of all things in God. It signifies that creation is imbued with divine meaning and awaits the human person to give voice to this meaning. Creation and humanity, we might say, are intended to form a symphony of divine praise and glory. In Bonaventure's view, the human person is the only one in creation who is capable of allowing that which already exists to be perfected in its existence by being led back to God. That is, the human person is the only one to recognize creation as the glory of God in the deepest sense of knowing the truth of that which exists, and the only one who can express this truth through prayerful uplifting of the heart to God. Through the human's recognition and expression of the divine imprint on created reality, everything in creation is led back to God.

The movement of *reductio* is integral to the spiritual journey which is based on the notion of the human person as image of God. As image, the human person is God-oriented and cannot find rest anywhere except in God. Originally, Bonaventure states, humans were created to know God within as image, as well as without, in the book of creation, and above, by the light of contemplation. However, sin distorted this image pushing the human person out into the darkness of the world. Wandering about aimlessly in the world, bent over by sin, the human person became disoriented within and without—in the depths of one's soul—and in the world of creation. Because of sin, the movement of *reductio* was thwarted and the relationship between God and creation was distorted. Although the human person is created as image of God, Bonaventure held that freedom is fundamental to the human person as image.[6] Herein is the axis of *reductio*. For it is only in freedom that the human person knows, recognizes and perfects whatever exists. Yet, because the human person is a *created* image of God, the freedom to be turned toward God is imperfect and dependent on grace. A deficiency in freedom underscores the ability to sin, to choose something other than God. And this is, indeed, what happened to humanity. Created as image but with the capacity to sin, the human person chose to be equal to God and the consequence of this choice was sin.

Because of sin, Bonaventure saw that the harmonious whole of God's creation became not only disrupted but fragmented, torn apart, throwing history onto a course of perilous ruin. Because God's goodness is absolute and his love totally communicative, however, God himself entered into history. The eternal Word of God, the origin of origins, took on our humanity so that God could reestablish the path of *reductio,* pointing out the destiny of things. As Bonaventure writes: "The eternal Word expresses the Father and at the same time the things that are created through Him."[7] Through Jesus Christ the profound structure of creation stands revealed. God the Father creates and sustains the world through the eternal Word and, in the incarnation, the Word enters into history to lead all things back to the Father.[8]

Bonaventure's emphasis on Christ the center is paramount to the whole of his vision. For he realizes that without this center, history has no real future promise. Only in Christ the center, the tree of life, can one return to God who is the source of life itself.[9] The relationship between Christ and humanity becomes the hinge of history's destiny, for all things are perfected in Christ insofar as they are transformed in his resurrection. Christ has led creation back to the Father but the movement of *reductio* is not yet complete. The human person who stands as image of Christ at the center of a fallen world must make the free choice to follow Christ as exemplar and Word. The relationship between freedom and the decision to follow Christ, therefore, is critical, for the movement of *reductio* is grounded in the human person's freedom. How we choose and what we choose determines our lives and the future of history in relation to God.[10] For Bonaventure, the Christian must choose Christ who shows himself as the Word of the Father to the believer. The unbeliever is not the person who does not know Christ but the one who *refuses* to recognize Christ as God hidden in the humble form of humanity. The believer is the one who desires God and, in receptivity to grace, turns toward God in Jesus Christ. Bonaventure never tires of emphasizing that only the humble can see the humble love of God poignantly expressed in the outstretched figure on the cross. For the person who chooses blindness, who refuses to recognize God in the poor and humble Christ, there is only the fate of history itself. In Bonaventure's view, humility, poverty and the cross form the basis of knowledge of the concrete truth that reveals the way. As he writes: "The cross is the key, the gate, the way, and the ray of truth."[11]

If Bonaventure was a realist he was also an optimist. The revelation of God in Christ who is exemplar, and the possibility of the world finding its unity in Christ through the human person, led him to view history with a horizon of hope. While some may claim today that the lack of peace and unity in the world reflect the failure of Christianity, others maintain that Christianity has not failed, it has never really been tried. Bonaventure, however, would not agree with the idea that Christianity has failed nor that it has never been tried. Rather, he saw Christianity as the hope of the world—not idealistically—but as concrete reality. For in the life of Francis he saw one who tried to be a Christian and succeeded. Although he held up Francis as the norm of Christian life (rather than simply as an exceptional human being), what he perceived in Francis is that *reductio* is possible because of the human person who is capable of union with God. There is hope, therefore, that history will progress toward a final age of peace and, ultimately, toward a final consummation in God because Francis attained this age of peace.

Bonaventure was aware, however, that Francis made a *free* choice to follow Christ who is the way to God. Freedom and identity, as Alexander Gerken points out, coinhere in Bonaventure's thought.[12] Because we are created in the Word of God and, as image, are oriented toward God, the human person cannot find the truth of oneself, that is, one's meaning and purpose, other than in God. And without coming to the truth of oneself, it is impossible to come to the truth of the world so as to lead it back to God. It is appropriate to say that the destiny of history depends on the human's search for identity. For when the question "who am I?" is asked, the poverty of the human person as radically dependent on God is revealed. This is the starting point for the journey to God, and once the human person embarks on the journey, so too is creation taken up in that journey to God. For Bonaventure, the search for identity prevails over every other aspect of human life. Although he himself must have been very gifted, Bonaventure was not interested in progress or human achievement; rather, he was concerned with ways in which humans use their gifts to find God. To be authentically human, in

Bonaventure's view, is more important than success or achievement which, apart from Christ, makes the human person into an idol and thus prevents the return of all things to God. Bonaventure's vision of the human person as the axis of historical transformation alerts us to the critical role humanity plays in the relationship between God and creation. Because this vision rests on the identity of the human person as image of God, it impels us to seek that center of unity in which the truth of our existence and the reason why we exist, find meaning in relation to God.

The search for meaning has never been more crucial than it is today as technology threatens to undermine the dignity of the human person. With the challenges of the new science and the complexities of a postmodern culture, the freedom to choose Christ as truth and life is becoming increasingly difficult. It is not unreasonable to say that the postmodern person is consumed with progress, success and achievement at the expense of authentic human identity. Becoming more alienated from the source of life, the contemporary person is losing touch with the pulse of life. The vast amount of information instantaneously available today stretches the postmodern person in various directions. Attracted by the marvels of technology which promise a better life, the human person is often torn apart from within quenched of energy by the lures of progress, frantically seeking identity in the face of pervasive alienation. The resurgence of interest in religion, the various forms of spirituality, including new age spirituality, and the desire to reconnect with the earth, all suggest that the twenty-first century person is in search of meaning and identity. Yet, the desire for authentic identity is thwarted by the very nature of the search itself, as people scramble through the overload of information via internet and mass communication to find an answer to their existential question, "who am I"? As Gerken states, the contemporary person has come to know more about things and less and less about him or her self—about what makes human persons unique and different.[13]

Bonaventure had a keen eye on the human condition and the mission and task of humans in the history of the world. He was not lured by the vast sources of uncontrolled power nor was he scathed by uncertainty and alienation. Rather, he was deeply aware that our origin, God, gives evidence of itself from within.[14] Interiority, by which the human image becomes ever the more illumined, means searching within for the fountain source of life. Bonaventure realized that the center of the soul is the center of the universe, namely, Jesus Christ; thus, the one who finds this center *within* finds this center at the heart of creation. It is because of this center that unity in the face of difference and diversity is possible. Christ, the center, is the one who mediates all opposites and unites them as mutually affirming complements. To truly enter within the soul where Christ is center is to become a source of unity in a world fragmented by differences.

Christians, enticed by the comfort and the success of achievement, however, are not impelled to search within, for the lure of success is intoxicating. The average person today works longer hours and relaxes less, partly driven by the need for money and partly conditioned by a culture that rewards success and marginalizes failure. In Bonaventure's view, prayer, solitude and the need to find God within require a slower pace of life and a certain prioritizing of values. A heart centered in God does not happen automatically. Rather, it is the work of disciplining one's habits, desires and pleasures. The desert fathers and mothers strove to acquire discipline of the body so that they could attain a heart centered in God. This, too, underscored the ascetical life of Francis. As Bonaventure wrote: "His flesh was in remarkable harmony with his spirit and his spirit with God."[15]

If the interior life is what brings us to this center of unity in which life finds its deepest meaning, Bonaventure was equally aware that a turning toward Christ in a personal relationship of love is what leads one into the center of the soul and into God. Such a relationship, in Bonaventure's view, is to make one passionate—not only on fire with the love of God—but consumed with the energy of life. Francis's passionate love of Christ was infectious not simply because he talked about it but because it shaped his entire being. All of his actions flowed out of this conviction. Despite the efforts today to renew Christian life, there are still many Christians who live without conviction and without passion. They are more excited about football than they are about Easter. They chant "Alleluia" while yawning and checking their watch. It is said that in the early church Christians prayed so loud their voices resonated beyond the walls of the church, throughout the villages, and the sound of the Christians praying inspired others to join them. If actions speak louder than words, it is reasonable that Christians who are passionless want to remain anonymous.

For Bonaventure, the Christian is not to be ashamed of knowing Christ and him crucified. Rather, the Christian is to rejoice in God's overflowing love revealed in Christ. Today, we hear among some Christians that it is better to remain publicly anonymous (as Christian) out of respect for other religions. Such a view simply vindicates the comfort of a private, bourgeois Christianity. For the idea of being an "anonymous Christian"[16] is an oxymoron. To be transformed in Christ and, in particular, Christ crucified, means that the very substance of one's life *is* Christ, and is expressed in the form of one's life. The name "Christian" expresses both the content of one's life and the form one's life takes which in some way must reflect the gospel life of Jesus Christ. For if one is truly a Christian one cannot be called by any other name;[17] it is an ontological reality, the essence of what one is as a human person and not merely the club one belongs to on Sunday or has professed membership in. In the early church, women and men were publicly executed because they refused to renounce their identity as "Christians." It is upon their blood that the Church we profess belief in remains. And this, too, is what Bonaventure maintains—the one who is truly a Christian is united to Christ and transformed in him in such a way that s/he cannot be called by any other name because Christ *is* the life that breathes through the person—the fire within that energizes his/her life. From a theological perspective, Bonaventure's notion of image and expression preempts anonymity because one cannot be an image of Christ without expressing this image in the form of one's life. Just as the Word expresses the Father, so too we are created to express the Word. The very content of *what* we are as image, therefore, shapes *who* we are as person. Because the person living in a relationship with Christ expresses this relationship in the totality of one's life, it is a contradiction to declare oneself as a Christian and, at the same time, remain publicly anonymous.

While privatized Christianity diminishes the mystery of Christ, it is being supplanted today by post-Christianity which, sensitive to a pluralistic culture, seeks to transcend Christ so as to live in a truly spiritual relationship to all people. To remove Christ from the center of life, however, is not only to remove the Word as the ground of being but it is to remove the Word as the ground of *reductio*. For when we remove the Word from our lives, we are no longer related to anything. It is only in the Word that we are truly united as brother and sister to every human person and to all the elements of creation. Thus, it is in and through the Word that *reductio* is completed. According to Bonaventure, the total expression of this Word in history and time is Christ, and only in Christ can one know the Word of God. Yet, there are some Christians today who are ashamed of Christ and try to excuse the historicity of the Incarnation. Perhaps it is because Christianity *is* a religion of historical significance that Christians feel the need to apologize to others and to find ways that circumvent the historical circumstances of Jesus' life. At this point, Christianity seems to be the only religion where the central figure of faith is an obstacle to practicing the religion. We do not hear Buddhists, for example, say, "Buddha is an obstacle for me to be compassionate to Christians," or Muslims say, "Allah is an obstacle for me to be merciful to Christians." It is because of Buddha and because of Allah that Buddhists and Muslims are compassionate and merciful people. And yet, the shamefulness of Christ goes further, to the suffering human figure on the cross.

Many Christians not only avoid the cross as the scandal of particularity but they fear the cross as a sign of suffering and failure. The cross is, undoubtedly, a public spectacle. And in a pluralistic world, Christians find it difficult to publicly profess that this crucified Jesus, who is the Christ, is the way, the truth and the life.

Although the one we believe to be God died a public shameful death on the cross, the story does not end here. If it did, Christianity would be a religion of violence and not a religion of life and, ultimately, eternal life. Bonaventure holds up the crucified Christ as our image in which we are to be transformed into the fire of God's love because Christ reigns eternally with the Father as *crucified and glorified*.[18] By the wounds he has suffered for us, he is victorious in love. Clare of Assisi understood this truth perfectly when she wrote:

> If you suffer with Him, you shall reign with Him,
> [if you] weep [with Him], you shall rejoice with Him;
> [if you] die [with Him] on the cross of tribulation,
> you shall possess heavenly mansions
> in the splendor of the saints
> and, in the Book of Life, your name shall be called
> glorious among people.[19]

The aim of the Christian life is to be victorious in love. It is this victory which undergirds the reduction of creation, the leading back of all things to God. And to be victorious in love, in Bonaventure's view, can only take place in union with Christ. Bonaventure sees the perfect expression of a loving relationship with Christ in the desire for martyrdom. How, we may ask, does this play out in daily Christian life? How does one *live* in a spirit of martyrdom? The key for Bonaventure is in our *spirit of desire.* To desire God in every aspect of life is to be turned to the other and willing to give to the other at the cost of oneself. Bonaventure describes this inner spirit as a "burning love"—it is a love that comes not from the duty of following the law; rather, it is a love that arises from a willingness to be transformed into the fire of God's love. The desert fathers and mothers with their keen insight to human nature emphasized inner transformation as the goal of the spiritual journey:

> Once upon a time, the story goes, Abba Lot went to see Abba Joseph. He said, "Abba, as much as I am able, I practice a small rule, all the little fasts, some prayer and meditation, and remain quiet. What else should I do?" To which the old monastic stood up and stretched his hands toward heaven, and his fingers became like ten torches of flame. And he said, "Why not be completely turned into fire?"[20]

This is a powerful story about human desire. How many of us wake up in the morning with the desire to be turned into fire? How many of us are so consumed by the fire of God's love that we are willing to suffer so as to be purified in love? Bonaventure frequently used the image of fire to describe the type of love the Christian must have if s/he truly desires God. "Listen Mother," he writes to a Poor Clare nun, "your heart is the altar of God. It is here that the fire of intense love must burn always."[21] Burning love is the love that enflames from within, "in one's very marrow," as Bonaventure writes; it is the fire of the Holy Spirit.[22] Such love cannot be hidden or anonymous for by its nature it radiates on the face of the believer.

If transformation of the human person is at the heart of Bonaventure's *reductio,* it is an essential transformation that does not come about apart from freedom, that is, a willingness to enter into the cross and to bear its consequences. God does not inflict suffering so as to force one to choose the cross. Rather, human freedom discloses the powerlessness of God, for God cannot violate that which flows out of God's goodness. Divine will, therefore, will always submit itself to gropings, to detours, even to revolts of human will to bring it to a free consent. God is a beggar of love waiting at the soul's door without ever daring to force it.[23] That is why the cross stands as the symbol of God's omnipotence, for it is God's power to love unconditionally. To freely choose Christ and him crucified underscores the conviction that Christ is truly God and worthy of the dedication of one's life. Only when this choice is present, according to Bonaventure, does the burning love of the Christian show itself in the willingness to suffer for the sake of love and ignite history from within, transforming it from apathy and indifference toward a God-intended future. To freely choose Christ goes hand in hand with the search for personal identity, that is, who we truly are in relation to God. The mystery of freedom and identity, which encapsulate Bonaventure's thought, is bound up with the mystery of Christ. For in freely choosing Christ, we not only come to the truth of our humanity but the mystery of Christ is born in us in such a way that the world becomes ever the more "Christic." We are responsible for the world, and it depends on us whether it blasphemes or prays. Only through us can the cosmos, like the body that it extends, receive grace.[24] We might say that Christ becomes the fullness of the universe when each of us lives in the fullness of Christ. Christ is the fountain-fullness of love at the center of the universe, and we embody that love when we come to the truth of our humanity in God. Becoming one in Christ is the realization of *reductio* because in Christ all things are restored and returned to the Father. The key to *reductio,* therefore, is freedom—how we choose and what we choose—as Christians. Upon this freedom history anticipates its future, creation embraces its destiny, humanity awaits its judgment and the Trinity—well—the Trinity simply continues to overflow in love.

Reflections

1. Do my choices reflect the mystery of my life, that I come from God, exist in God and am returning to God?

2. How do I understand my Christian identity? How significant is it to me? What prevents me from living an authentic Christian life? What needs to grow/change?

3. Read and pray using John 11:1–44. In what areas of my life am I confined or bound? Does my use of freedom help or hinder my life in God?

4. Where or in what do I seek my completion? In God or things other than God? What insight does this call me to? Ask God, who is burning love, to purify and increase your faith.

Notes

1. According to Jacques Bougerol (*Introduction to Works of Bonaventure*, 132), Bonaventure addressed his series of lectures to the Franciscan friars and others at Paris between April 9 and May 28 of the year 1273.

2. *Hex.* 1.17 (V, 332). "[Hoc est medium *metaphysicum* reducens], et haec est tota nostra metaphysica: de emanatione, de exemplaritate, de consummatione, scilicet illuminari per radios spirituales et reduci ad summum."

3. *Hex.* 1.17 (V, 332); *Hex.* 10.12–14 (V, 378); *Red. art.* 7 (V, 332). In the drama of creation Bonaventure distinguishes three main phases: the *emanatio*, the *exemplaritas*, and the *consummatio* which is also called *reductio*. The meaning of these phases is that the created world as a whole and all creatures in this world have their origin in God from whom they proceed; having been created, they reflect God, their divine model or exemplar; they finally return to God for whom they were created and who is their ultimate end. These three phases are closely connected with one another and form one continuous line or process. Since this line returns to the same point from which it began, it forms a circular movement. However, if the line of creation does not bend back and close on its beginning, it has not found its perfection. See Hayes, commentary on "Sermon II on the Nativity," in *What Manner of Man*, 93, nn. 45–46.

4. *Hex.* 13.12 (V, 390) "Certum est, quod homo stans habebat cognitionem rerum creatarum et per illarum repraesentationem ferebatur in Deum ad ipsum laudandum, venerandum, amandum; et ad hoc sunt creaturae et sic reducuntur in Deum." In his third lecture (*Hex.* 3.2 [V, 343]), Bonaventure states that unless we are able to view things in terms of how they originate, how they are to be reduced to their end,

and how God shines forth in them, we will never be able to understand, that is, come to the truth of things. For a discussion on emanation and reduction in Bonaventure's thought, see Hayes, *Center*, 12–13; Bowman, "Cosmic Exemplarism," 195–98.

5. Francis of Assisi "The Canticle of the Creatures." Engl. trans. FA:ED I, 114.

6. In his *Breviloquium*, Bonaventure describes the soul as a "form endowed with freedom." He indicates that in the state of innocence, the soul was free from misery and sin, but not so in the fallen state. The soul is free from compulsion, however, insofar as the intellect and will are able to freely choose God. He writes: "Freedom of choice is a power of both reason and will. . . . The cooperation of these two faculties—reason reflecting upon itself and will acting in conjunction—gives rise to full freedom, the source of merit or demerit accordingly as good or evil is chosen." *Brev.* 2.9.1.8 (V, 226b–227b). Engl. trans. De Vinck, *Breviloquium*, 93, 97.

7. *Hex.* 1.17 (V, 332). Engl. trans. De Vinck, *Six Days of Creation*, 9.

8. Alexander Gerken, "Identity and Freedom: Bonaventure's Position and Method," trans. Myles Parsons, *Greyfriars Review* 4 (1990); 101; Hayes makes a similar point in his discussion of a Christocentric metaphysics. See Hayes, "Christology and Metaphysics," S92.

9. *Hex.* 1.17 (V, 332).

10. Gerken, "Identity and Freedom," 101.

11. *Tripl. via.* 3.5 (VIII, 14). "Unde ipsa crux est clavis, porta, via et splendor veritatis, quam qui tollit et sequitur iuxta modum praeassignatum non ambulat in tenebris, sed habebit lumen vitae."

12. Gerken ("Identity and Freedom," 96–105) sees identity and freedom as the two main pillars of Bonaventure's thought that undergird *reductio* and, we might add, provide a theological basis to Bonaventure's historical consciousness.

13. Ibid., 104.

14. Ibid., 105. Gerken provides profound insight to Bonaventure's meaning of *reductio* indicating that Bonaventure is no mere dreamer. As he writes: "The ground that Bonaventure has trod is by no means a mere look backwards, merely a conservative posture. He points to the future. He is aware of the mission and task of the human person in the history of the world."

15. *Leg. maj.* 5.9 (EM, 45). Engl. trans. FA:ED II, 567.

16. Karl Rahner used the term "anonymous Christian" to describe people outside the faith who, unaware of Christ, exhibit Christian attitudes and values. However, I am not using the term in this way. Rather, I am using it in a more literal sense of Christians who want to remain publicly anonymous precisely as Christian.

17. The commitment to being Christian was evident in the early church martyrs. Simply by declaring oneself a Christian, one could be sent to his/her death in the arena. For an inspiring account of a young

martyr who refused to be called by any other name other than Christian, see the martyrdom account of "The Passion of Perpetua and Felicitas," in *Medieval Women's Visionary Literature*, ed. Elizabeth Petroff (New York: Oxford University Press, 1986), 70–77.

18. See *Lig. vit.* 38 (VIII, 82).

19. Clare of Assisi "The Second Letter to Agnes of Prague," 21–22, in *Francis and Clare*, 197.

20. *Sayings of the Desert Fathers*, Joseph of Panephysis 7 quoted in *Lives of the Desert Fathers*, trans. Benedicta Ward (London: Mowbray, 1980), 45.

21. *Perf. vit.* 6.1 (VIII, 120). Engl. trans. De Vinck, "Perfection of Life," 239.

22. *Itin.* 7.4 (V, 312).

23. Vladimir Lossky, *Orthodox Theology: An Introduction* (New York: St. Vladimir's Seminary Press, 1978), 73.

24. Ibid., 71.

Excerpts of Bonaventure's Writings

A Note on the Writings

Bonaventure's writings are extensive, covering approximately nine folio volumes in the Quaracchi critical edition, with the individual volumes averaging over seven hundred pages, printed in double columns.[1] His works can be classified under three general headings: scholastic treatises, spiritual writings and lectures.[2] A fourth category would include his writings concerning the Franciscan Order. Since these are a mixture of spirituality and prescriptions for Franciscan life, however, it is difficult to classify them as a particular category of writings. I include them, therefore, under the more general category of spiritual writings.

The first set of writings, the scholastic treatises, are works of the academy produced during Bonaventure's tenure at the University of Paris. These works were written between the years 1248 and 1257. As a student at the University, Bonaventure was trained in the method of disputed questions, a rigorous pattern of analysis by which a question was "objectively" answered. The thoroughly scientific nature of this type of reasoning undergirds Bonaventure's commentary on the *Sentences*, as well as his disputed questions on the *Mystery of the Trinity*, *Knowledge of Christ* and *Evangelical Perfection*.

The second type of writings, the spiritual writings, were composed by Bonaventure after his departure from the University in 1257 whereupon he assumed the role as Minister General. It is not unlikely that as Minister General of a large and diffuse Order, Bonaventure searched for clarity on the meaning of being Christian and Franciscan. His letters to the Poor Clare nuns indicate that his "care of souls" was not limited to friars alone but to nuns and probably lay people as well. Bonaventure's spiritual writings clearly had an influence beyond the boundaries of the Franciscans. George Marcil states that the *Tree of Life*, for example, represented a new departure in the trend in spirituality stressing the imitation of Christ.[3] John Fleming states that the poetical and lyrical style which is characteristic of the *Tree of Life* stimulated an artistic movement that eventually spread Franciscan devotional elements throughout Europe.[4] Similarly, Sandro Sticca claimed that Bonaventure's devotional writings constituted a homiletic trend toward pietism and human realism with an emphasis on Christ's earthly life and sufferings.[5] It is apparent, therefore, that Bonaventure's spiritual writings were neither merely devotional exercises nor pious exhortations to boost the spiritual temperature of the Franciscans. Rather, they were works with profound import for the whole of medieval spirituality, ultimately influencing the arts, literature and drama.

Closely related to his spiritual writings are Bonaventure's writings concerning the Franciscan Order, including the "Constitutions of Narbonne" which decisively shaped the ideals and life of the brotherhood.[6] As Minister General, Bonaventure was charged with the responsibility of ensuring the integrity of the Franciscan life both in its spiritual and intellectual development. Whether writing instructions for novices or guidelines for the Order, the writings of the Minister General were deeply spiritual and reflected his search for identity. His wide range of correspondence indicated that his pivotal position was one of mediation between the Franciscan Order and various ecclesiastical authorities. While the writings concerning the Order are prescriptive, many of them are spiritual directives on Franciscan life.

Although Bonaventure's spiritual writings were produced during the time of his Generalate, between 1259 and 1273, he continued to maintain ties with the University of Paris. The influx of Latin Aristotelianism into the intellectual mainstream impelled the Seraphic Doctor to defend the foundation of Christian doctrine. He did this in his series of lectures (*collationes*) which were recorded by students in attendance. These lectures were given at several different times: in 1267 on the *Ten Commandments*, in 1268 on the *Gifts of the Holy Spirit* and in 1273 on the *Six Days of Creation*.

In a sense, these three periods of works reflect the three "lives" of Bonaventure: the theologian, the mystic and the Christian leader. The samples of Bonaventure's writings presented here are arranged in chronological order to illustrate these various "lives" or voices Bonaventure assumed as he sought to clarify the meaning of Christian life on all levels. Together they bear witness to one of the most remarkable scholars and saints of the Middle Ages, a person illumined by the brilliance of divine light and flooded by divine love. As Gerken points out, Bonaventure lived with an impassioned quest for identity, and this quest pervaded the entirety of his work.[7] With a passion for truth and for the meaning of human existence, Bonaventure never tired of exploring the God of infinite love. He is, without doubt, one of the great lights of the thirteenth century.

Notes

1. Ewert Cousins, introduction to *Bonaventure*, 8.
2. Ibid.
3. George Marcil, "Contrasting St. Bonaventure's *Tree of Life* and the *Meditations on the Life of Christ*," *Cord* 32 (1982): 327.
4. John Fleming, *An Introduction to the Franciscan Literature of the Middle Ages* (Chicago: Franciscan Herald Press, 1977), 210; Harry B Gutman, "The Rebirth of the Fine Arts and Franciscan Thought," *Franciscan Studies* 25 (1945): 215–24.
5. Sandro Sticca, "*Officium Passionis Domini*: An Unpublished Manuscript of the Fourteenth Century," *Franciscan Studies* 34 (1974): 156.
6. Monti, *Writings Concerning the Franciscan Order*, 71.
7. Gerken, "Identity and Freedom," 94–5.

Whether the Human Person is Truly an Image of God

We will proceed thus and show that the human person is truly an image of God.

a. Gn 1:26: "Let us make human persons in our image," etc. This is nothing else than a statement by the Trinity. Therefore, etc.

b. Also, Eccl 17:1: "God created human persons from the earth and made them in his own image." If, then, human persons are made in the image of God, they are the image of God.

c. Also, what is by its nature especially constituted to be united with another, is by its nature especially constituted to be similar to the other in form and figure. For love, since it unites, is said to transform the lover into the beloved, as Hugh says. But a rational creature, such as the human person, is by his/her nature especially constituted to be united with God and to strive toward God through love. Therefore s/he is by his/her nature especially constituted to be like and similar to him. If, then, image signifies an expressed likeness, it is clear, etc.

d. Also, what represents something in its noble act and in distinction and order is truly its image. But the human person truly represents God in his or her most noble act, which is to understand. For he or she not only represents God insofar as one exists and is alive, but also insofar as he or she is intelligent. Also, the

> human person represents God in his or her distinction and order, which is in persons, in one's memory, understanding and will. Therefore, the human person is truly an image of God.

To understand what was said above, it should be noted that image means expressed likeness. Now it is necessary that every creature be like God in some way. It is also necessary for the completion of the universe that some creature be like God expressly. Therefore every creature has the character of vestige but some creatures have the character of image, those, namely, that are expressly like God. Now these are rational creatures, such as human persons. Therefore we must concede that the human person is an image of God because s/he is God's expressed likeness. . . .

And this is clear in the following way. First, concerning convergence in ordering. For "God has made all things for himself" in such a way that, since he is the supreme power and majesty, he made all things to praise himself; since he is the supreme light, he made all things to manifest himself; since he is the supreme goodness, he made all things to communicate himself. But there is no perfect praise unless there is someone present to approve; nor perfect manifestation unless there is someone present to understand; nor perfect communication of goods unless there is someone present to put them to use. Only a rational creature has the capacity to approve praise, to know truth, and to accept gifts for his/her use. Therefore, non-rational creatures do not have to be ordered to God immediately but by means of rational creatures. But since rational creatures are by nature constituted to praise and know and to accept other things into their faculty of will, they are by nature ordered to God immediately. And the more immediately something is ordered to something else, the more it converges with it in the convergence of ordering. The rational soul, as well as any rational creature, insofar as it is capable of God and can participate in him, is immediately ordered to him. Therefore, it converges with him in the highest degree with the convergence of ordering. And since the greater the convergence, the more expressed is the likeness, it follows that, in respect to this kind of likeness, a rational creature is an expressed likeness and, therefore, an image. And this is what Augustine says [*De trinitate* 15.8.11], "the soul is an image of God by the fact that it is capable of him and can partake in him." And because "it is capable of him and can partake in him" it is, by its nature, constituted to be similar to him and, moreover, bears within itself, from its origin, the light of the divine countenance. Therefore, regarding the likeness that refers to convergence in ordering, it is with perfect accuracy called an image of God because, in this respect, it is expressly like God.

II *Sentences* d. 16, a. 1, q. 1, concl.
(ca. 1250–1252)

Translated by Ewert Cousins

Primacy and Trinity

Supreme primacy in the supreme and highest principle demands the highest actuality, the highest fontality, and the highest fecundity. For the first principle, by virtue of the fact that it is first, is the most perfect in production, the most fontal in emanating, and the most fecund in germinating. Therefore since the perfect production, emanation and germination is realized only through two intrinsic modes, namely, by way of nature and by way of will, that is by way of the word and of love, therefore the highest perfection, fontality, and fecundity necessarily demands two kinds of emanation with respect to the two hypostases which are produced and emanate from the first person as from the first producing principle. Therefore, it is necessary to affirm three persons. And since the most perfect production is not realized except with respect to equals, and the most fontal emanation is not realized except with respect to co-eternals, and the most fecund germination is not realized except with respect to consubstantial beings, it is necessary to admit that the first principle includes within itself three hypostases that are coequal, coeternal, and consubstantial. The primacy of the first principle, therefore, demands the most perfect trinity in order, origin, and distinction; of coequality, coeternity, and consubstantiality; it demands also the highest unity, simplicity, immensity, eternity, immutability, and actuality. Therefore, it requires a trinity in the first principle together with the above-mentioned essential qualities.

Therefore, since the first principle, by virtue of the fact that it is the first being, is supremely one; and for this reason it is supremely simple and immense; and for the same reason it is eternal, unchangeable, and necessary as may be gathered from above; and again, by the mere fact that it is the first being, it is most perfect in producing, most fontal in emanating, and most fecund in germinating, and this with respect to things that are equal, coeternal, consubtantial, distinct, original, and ordered, it follows that the first principle, because it is first, exists eternally with the fullness of all these perfect qualities. For this reason, it is in this principle, in as far as it is first, that all beings and all knowledge come to rest. . . .

But if a being is said to be first because of the lack of origin, that is, because it does not take its origin from another, in this sense, primacy resides principally in the person of the Father; and for this reason, the fontal-fullness for the production of all the persons is found in Him. Hence, because innascibility includes this property, the notion of the Father is said to be a property. But this would not be the case unless it simultaneously involved perfection and the cause of manifestation; also, it would be predicated in a relative sense.

To the objection that they are either equally active as principle or they are not, it must be said that they are equally principle in the order of essence but not in the order of person; for the Father is principle of two persons; the Son is principle of one; and the Holy Spirit is principle of none. Therefore, since that primacy which is proper to the first principle in the order of essence is found equally in all three persons, the trinity exists together with supreme primacy; because, just as "not to be able to generate" involves no impotence in the Son, so "not to exist from oneself, but from the Father" involves no posteriority and therefore does not diminish the perfect primacy.

To the objection that the more a being is fontal, the more it is prior in producing, it must be said that—as we have already seen—the first being may be understood in two ways; by way of the lack of essential anteriority, and by way of the lack of personal origin. Thus, it includes a two-fold fontality depending on whether it refers to the lack of esential anteriority or to the lack of personal origin. When it is taken to mean the lack of essential anteriority, it includes fontality with respect to the effects and essences to be produced. Thus, since this condition is equally fitting to all the persons, it is equally proper to all of them to possess the nature of fontality in the production of created beings, since they are not three but one principle of creation. But in as far as it involves the lack of personal origin, it befits only that person who is innascible; namely, the Father in whom resides the fullness of fontality for the production of the Son and the Holy Spirit.

And, in a certain way, this sort of fontality is the origin of the other fontality. For, since the Father brings forth the Son, and through the Son, and together with the Son brings forth the Holy Spirit, God the Father through the Son and with the Holy Spirit is the principle of everything created; for if He did not produce them eternally, He could not produce through anything in time; and therefore He is rightly called the "Fount of Life" by reason of this production within the trinity. "As He has life in Himself, so He grants to the Son to have life in Himself," etc. Therefore it follows that eternal life consists in this alone, that the rational spirit, which emanates from the most blessed trinity and is a likeness of the trinity, should return after the manner of a certain intelligible circle—through memory, intelligence, and will—to the most blessed trinity by God-conforming glory.

M. Trin. q. 8, concl.
(ca. 1253)

Translated by Zachary Hayes
Disputed Questions on the Mystery of the Trinity, vol. 3
Works of Saint Bonaventure, ed. George Marcil
(St. Bonaventure, NY: The Franciscan Institute, 1979), 263–65.

A Letter to the Abbess and Sisters of Saint Clare in Assisi

Brother Bonaventure, General Minister and servant of the Order of Friars Minor, to his dearly beloved daughters in Christ Jesus, the Abbess of the Poor Ladies of Assisi in the monastery of St. Clare, and to all her sisters: greetings! With those other blessed virgins prepared [for his wedding feast], may you *follow the Lamb wherever he goes*.

My dear daughters in the Lord, when recently I learned from our dearest brother Leo, one time companion of our holy Father, how intent you are on serving the poor crucified Christ in all purity, as spouses of the eternal King, I rejoiced greatly in the Lord because of it. I now wish through this letter to offer every encouragement to this devotion of yours, so that you might follow earnestly the virtuous footprints of your holy Mother, who was instructed by the Holy Spirit through that little poor man, Saint Francis. "May you never wish to have anything else under heaven except what your Mother taught, namely *Jesus Christ, and him crucified*. After her example, hasten, dear daughters, after the fragrance of his blood. Boldly take hold of the mirror of poverty, the pattern of humility, the shield of endurance, the insignia of obedience. Then, enkindled by the fire of divine love, give your heart totally to the one who on the cross offered himself to God the Father for us. For insofar as you are clothed in the light of your Mother's example, on fire with those delightful flames which burn perpetually, and redolent of the perfume of every virtue, you will become the *aroma of Christ*, the Virgin's Son and the Spouse of wise virgins, *among those who are being saved and among those who are perishing*.

Be so attentive in maintaining those desires and so fervent in the spirit of devotion, that when the *cry is raised, "Here is the bridegroom!"* the lamps of your souls will already be filled with the oil of love and joy, so that you may go forth to meet him happily. While the foolish virgins are left outside, you will enter with him to the wedding banquet of eternal gladness. There Christ will *have* his spouses *sit down* with his angels and elect *and will come and serve them*, offering them the *bread of life*, the flesh of the *Lamb slain*, and *fish broiled* on the cross, cooked on the fire of his love, that burning passion with which he loved you. Then he *will give you wine to drink, mulled* with his humanity and divinity; from this cup his friends drink deeply, till, marvelously sober, they are drunk with love. Thus you will go on and on enjoying that *goodness laid up for those who fear* him. You will gaze constantly upon the one who is not only *the most handsome of men*, but fairest also among the myriads of angels. Why, he is the one whom *the angels long to glimpse*; for he is *the reflection of eternal light, the flawless mirror of the majesty of God and the image of his goodness.* And so, my beloved daughters, as you continually cling to Christ as our everlasting good, and when he blesses you with his favors, commend me, a sinner, to his ineffable mercy. Keep up your prayers, so that for the glory and honor of his marvelous name, he would be kind enough to *keep my steps steady* in caring for the poor little flock of Christ which has been entrusted to me.

Given on the holy mountain of La Verna.

(ca. 1259)

Translated by Dominic Monti
Writings Concerning the Franciscan Order, vol. 5
Works of Saint Bonaventure, ed. George Marcil
(St. Bonaventure, NY: The Franciscan Institute, 1994), 68–70.

From the Prologue to the Tree of Life

Picture in your mind a tree whose roots are watered by an ever-flowing fountain that becomes a great and living river with four channels to water the garden of the entire Church. From the trunk of this tree, imagine that there are growing twelve branches that are adorned with leaves, flowers and fruit. Imagine that the leaves are a most effective medicine to prevent and cure every kind of sickness, because the word of the cross *is the power of God for salvation to everyone who believes* (Rom 1:16). Let the flowers be beautiful with the radiance of every color and perfumed with the sweetness of every fragrance, awakening and attracting the anxious hearts of people of desire. Imagine that there are twelve fruits, *having every delight and the sweetness of every taste* (Wis 16:20). This fruit is offered to God's servants to be tasted so that when they eat it, they may always be satisfied, yet never grow weary of its taste. This is the fruit that took its origin from the Virgin's womb and reached its savory maturity on the tree of the cross under the midday heat of the Eternal Sun, that is, the love of Christ. In the garden of the heavenly paradise—God's table—this fruit is served to those who desire it. This is suggested by the first stanza, which says: O cross, salvation-bearing tree, watered by a living fountain, your flower is spice-scented, your fruit an object of desire.

Although this fruit is one and undivided, it nourishes devout souls with varied consolations in view of its varied states, excellence, powers and works. These can be reduced to twelve. This fruit of the tree of life, therefore, is pictured and is offered to our taste under twelve flavors on twelve branches. On the first branch the soul devoted to Christ perceives the flavor of sweetness, by recalling the distinguished origin and sweet birth of her Savior; on the second branch, the humble mode of life which he condescended to adopt; on the third, the loftiness of his perfect power; on the fourth, the plenitude of his most abundant piety; on the fifth, the confidence which he had in the trial of his passion; on the sixth, the patience which he exhibited in bearing great insults and injuries; on the seventh, the constancy which he maintained in the torture and suffering of his rough and bitter cross; on the eighth, the victory which he achieved in the conflict and passage of death; on the ninth, the novelty of his resurrection embellished with remarkable gifts; on the tenth, the sublimity of his ascension, pouring fourth spiritual charisms; on the eleventh, the equity of the future judgment; on the twelfth, the eternity of the divine kingdom.

I call these fruits because they delight with their rich sweetness and strengthen with their nourishment the soul who meditates on them and diligently considers each one, abhoring the example of the unfaithful Adam who preferred *the tree of the knowledge of good and evil* (Gn 2:17) to the tree of life. No one can avoid this error unless s/he prefers faith to reason, devotion to investigation, simplicity to curiosity and finally the sacred cross of Christ to all carnal feeling or wisdom of the flesh. Through the cross the charity of the Holy Spirit is nourished in devout hearts and the sevenfold grace is poured fourth, as is requested in the two first and last verses.

(ca. 1260)

Translated by Ewert Cousins
Bonaventure: The Soul's Journey Into God, The Tree of Life
The Life of St. Francis
(New York: Paulist Press, 1978), 120–22.

On the Third Commandment of the Decalogue: Collation IV

There are three things which are required for perfect love. The first is the divine rest which directs the soul to God. The second is the imitation of Christ in good works. The third is the abstention from all servile work, which renders the heart pure and clean.

The turning of a soul back to God is accomplished by means of seven works. Without these works the soul is not turned toward perfect rest in God. Three of these are interior and are done by meditating, by praying and by praising. And from these three comes contemplation. The other four are exterior and are accomplished by reading, by singing the psalms, by offering sacrifice and by fulfilling the divine law. And this is done either by hearing or by teaching, or by conferring with others.

And this is why it says: "Remember to keep holy the Sabbath day." Therefore the Lord first commands a rest in which the soul can turn toward God.

Secondly, God commands the imitation of himself by saying: "Six days you will labor." Of that imitation the Apostle says: "Be imitators of God as dearest children," and in Luke it says: "Be merciful even as your Father is merciful."

There are six works of mercy: to feed the hungry, to give drink to the thirsty, to clothe the naked, to care for the stranger, to visit the sick and to ransom the captive. A work of perfect virtue is not possible unless a creature is conformed to Christ in these things.

Six things are required to do a work of virtue, corresponding to the works of the six days of creation. These are: provident consideration, right intention, pure affection, just or correct choice, a vigorous carrying out and a putting on of love. The first is understood in the work of the first day, when God said: "Let there be light," and there was light. This is provident consideration.

Secondly, one should direct oneself to the right end in God. This is noted when it says: "Let there be a firmament in the midst of the waters, and God called the firmament heaven," because one should be directed heavenwards, so as to have a right intention with respect to God.

Thirdly, pure affection is required. This is what is understood in the third work when God divided the land from the water, thus separating worldly affections from divine affections.

Fourthly, a just or correct choice is required, so that all our works might be done in an orderly way, as they should be. This is noted in the fourth work, when it says: "Let there be lights in the firmament of the heaven," that is, let our works be ordered.

Fifthly, a vigorous carrying out is required. This is noted in the fifth work, when God produced living beings in the water, such as fish, and in the air, such as birds.

Sixthly, a putting on the form of love is required, so that the works might be complete, prepared for all circumstances according to the demands of the law of divine love. For love is the perfect form of all things, and the one who has love has all six requirements. So the sixth work is the putting on of love. This is noted when it says: "God made man in the image and likeness of himself." When the work of a human person brings together these six elements, then it is said the person lives rightly.

Collationes de decem praeceptis 4.12–14
(ca. 1267)

Translated by Paul J. Spaeth
St. Bonaventure's Collations on the Ten Commandments, vol. 6
Works of Saint Bonaventure, ed. F. Edward Coughlin
(St. Bonaventure, New York: The Franciscan Institute, 1995), 66–68.

First Collation on the Six Days of Creation

10. As regards the second point, note that a beginning should be made from the center (*medium*), that is, from Christ. For he himself is the *mediator between God and humanity* (1 Tm 2:5) and holds the central position in all things, as shall be seen. Thus, a person who wishes to attain Christian wisdom must start from him. This fact is proved in [the Gospel according to] Matthew (11:27): "*For no one knows the Son except the Father; nor does anyone know the Father except the Son, and the one to whom the Son chooses to reveal Him.*"

It is also evident that a person should begin with the One from whom the two greatest wise men began: Moses, the initiator of God's wisdom, and John, its consummator. The former said: *In the beginning God created the heavens and the earth* (Gn 1:1) and, according to Augustine, this means "in the Son." And John (1:1) said: *In the beginning was the Word, and the Word was with God; and the Word was God. He was in the beginning with God. All things were made through him*. If, therefore, one can truly understand a creature only by [knowing] the reality by which it was made, it is necessary that *the true Word go before you* (cf. Sir 37:20).

11. Our intent, then, is to show that in Christ *are hidden all the treasures of wisdom and knowledge* (Col 2:3), and that he himself is the center of all [forms of] knowledge. For he is the center in seven different ways: according to essence, nature, distance, doctrine, moderation, justice, and concord. The first pertains to the concern of the metaphysician; the second, the [physical] scientist; the third, the mathematician; the fourth, the logician; the fifth, the moralist; the sixth, the politician or the jurist; and the seventh, the theologian. The first center is primary by its eternal origin, the second is most strong through the diffusion of its power, the third is most profound

because of the centrality of its position, the fourth is most clear by its rational proof, the fifth is most important because of the choice of moral goodness, the sixth is outstanding because of the retribution of justice, the seventh is peaceful through its universal reconciliation. Christ was the first center by his eternal generation; the second by his incarnation; the third through his passion; the fourth by his resurrection; the fifth by his ascension; the sixth in his future judgment; the seventh in eternal retribution or beatification. . . .

12–14. And so, the first center is in the order of essence. It is first by reason of eternal generation. . . . For from all eternity the Father begets a Son similar to himself, and in him expresses his true likeness, and in so doing he has expressed all his [active] potency. [In him] he has expressed everything he can do and, most of all, what he wishes to do. Thus all things have been expressed in him, his Son—in that center, which so to speak is his art. . . .

15. Of this center, it is said in Genesis (2:9): *The Lord God made to grow from the earth all types of trees beautiful to look at and pleasant to eat, with the tree of life in the center of paradise*. Accordingly, Augustine said that of everything that was created it was said [in Genesis]: *Let it be done; God made it; and it was made*—except light, of which it is said [only]: *"Let there be light," and there was light*. This is because all these [other] things were produced first of all from all eternity, in the eternal art; then, in the intelligent creature; and finally, in the sensible world.

16. This passage opposes the errors of those who believe the world was created from eternity. For arguing that our minds came into being with the eternal lights, they maintain that just as things were eternally brought forth [in the Word] or written in the eternal art, so too they were created in the material world from all eternity. Thus, [they argue that] this world, which is written in the eternal art from all eternity, has also been eternally written out in matter. But this passage from Genesis concerning the earthly paradise concerns angelic, human, and eternal intelligences. Thus, it says in effect, that the Father begot One like himself, the Word who is coeternal

with him and bears his likeness, and consequently in this Word he expressed everything, all that he was able to do.

17–18. Hence this Word expresses the Father and *the things he has made through him* (Jn 1:3), and this beginning leads us to union with the Father who brings all things together. In this way he is the *Tree of Life* (Gn 2.9), for through this means (center) we return to the very *fountain of life* (Ps 34:10). . . . Such a One is the metaphysical center that leads us back [to God], and such a One sums up our metaphysics: emanation, exemplarity, and consummation—that is to say, to be illumined by rays of spiritual light and to return to the Most High. In this way, you will be a true metaphysician.

Collationes in Hexaëmeron 1.10–17
(ca. 1273)

Translated by Ilia Delio, Timothy Johnson
and Dominic Monti

Select Bibliography

Critical Editions

Bonaventure. *Doctoris Seraphici S. Bonaventurae Opera Omnia.* Edited by PP. Collegii Sancti Bonaventurae. 10 Vols. Ad Aquas, Quaracchi: Collegium Sancti Bonaventurae, 1882–1902.

———. *Legenda maior S. Francisci Assisiensis et eiusdem Legenda minor.* Edited by PP. Collegii Sancti Bonaventurae. (Editio minor) Ad Aquas, Quaracchi: Collegium Sancti Bonaventurae, 1941.

———. *Collationes in Hexaëmeron et Bonaventuriana quaedam selecta.* Edited by Ferdinand Delorme. Quaracchi: Collegii Sancti Bonaventurae, 1934.

Primary Works

Angela of Foligno. *Angela of Foligno: Complete Works.* Introduction and translation by Paul Lachance. New York: Paulist Press, 1993.

Armstrong, Regis J. and Ignatius Brady, trans. *Francis and Clare: The Complete Works.* New York: Paulist Press, 1982.

———., J. A. Wayne Hellmann, and William J. Short. eds. *Francis of Assisi: Early Documents.* Vol. 1, *The Saint,* vol. 2, *The Founder,* vol. 3, *The Prophet.* Hyde Park, NY: New City Press, 1999–2001.

Bonaventure. *On the Reduction of Arts to Theology.* Introduction and translation by Zachary Hayes. Vol. 1, *Works of Saint Bonaventure.* Edited by F. Edward Coughlin. St. Bonaventure, New York: The Franciscan Institute, 1996.

———. *Collations on the Ten Commandments.* Introduction and translation by Paul J. Spaeth. Vol. 6, *Works of Saint Bonaventure.* Edited by F. Edward Coughlin. St. Bonaventure, New York: The Franciscan Institute, 1995.

———. *Disputed Questions on the Knowledge of Christ.* Introduction and translation by Zachary Hayes. Vol. 4, *Works of Saint Bonaventure.* Edited by George Marcil. St. Bonaventure, New York: The Franciscan Institute, 1992.

———. *Disputed Questions on the Mystery of the Trinity*. Introduction and translation by Zachary Hayes. Vol. 3, *Works of Saint Bonaventure*. Edited by George Marcil. St. Bonaventure, New York: The Franciscan Institute, 1979.

———. *St. Bonaventure's Writings Concerning the Franciscan Order*. Introduction and translation by Dominic Monti. Vol 5, *Works of Saint Bonaventure*. Edited by George Marcil. St. Bonaventure, New York: The Franciscan Institute, 1994.

———. Works of Bonaventure. Translated by José de Vinck. 5 Vols. Paterson: St. Anthony Guild Press, 1960–1970.

Bougerol, Jacques-Guy, ed. *Lexique Saint Bonaventure*. Paris: Éditions Franciscaines, 1969.

Cousins, Ewert, trans. *Bonaventure: The Soul's Journey Into God, The Tree of Life, The Life of St. Francis*. New York: Paulist Press, 1978.

Desbonnet, Théophile, Thaddée Matura, Jean-François Godet, Damien Vorreux, intro. and trans. *François d'Assise. Écrits*. Vol. 285, *Sources Chrétiennes*. Paris: Éditions Franciscaines, 1981.

Doyle Eric, ed. And trans. *Disciple and the Master: St. Bonaventure's Sermons on St. Francis of Assisi*. Chicago: Franciscan Herald Press, 1983.

Hayes, Zachary. *What Manner of Man? Sermons on Christ by St. Bonaventure*. Chicago: Franciscan Herald Press, 1989.

Johnson, Timothy, ed. *Bonaventure: Mystic of God's Word*. Hyde Park, NY: New City Press, 1999.

Pseudo-Dionysius. *Pseudo-Dionysius: The Complete Works*. Translated by Colm Luibheid. New York: Paulist Press, 1987.

Richard of St. Victor. *De trinitate. Patrologia Latina* 196, 887–992.

———. *Selected Writings on Contemplation*. Translation and introduction by Clare Kirchberger. London: Faber and Faber, 1957.

Secondary Works

de Asis Chavero Blanco, Francisco, ed. *Bonaventuriana. Miscellanea in onore di Jacques-Guy Bougerol*. 2 Vols. Rome: Edizioni Antonianum, 1988.

Bissen, Jean-Marie. *L'exemplarisme divin selon saint Bonaventure*. Paris: J. Vrin, 1929.

Bougerol, Jacques-Guy, ed. *Bonaventura, Sancti 1274–1974*. 5 Vols. Grottaferrata: Collegii S. Bonaventurae, 1973–74.

———. *Introduction to the Works of Bonaventure*. Translated by José de Vinck. Paterson, New Jersey: St. Anthony Guild Press, 1964.

Carpenter, Charles. *Theology As the Road to Holiness in Saint Bonaventure*. New York: Paulist Press, 1999.

Cousins, Ewert. *Bonaventure and the Coincidence of Opposites*. Chicago: Franciscan Herald Press, 1978.

Daniel, E. Randolph. *The Franciscan Concept of Mission in the High Middle Ages*. Lexington: University of Kentucky Press, 1975.

Delio, Ilia. *Crucified Love: Bonaventure's Mysticism of the Crucified Christ*. Quincy, IL: Franciscan Press, 1998.

Fleming, John. *An Introduction to the Franciscan Literature of the Middle Ages*. Chicago: Franciscan Herald Press, 1977.

Gerken, Alexander. *Théologie du Verbe: La relation entre l'incarnation et la création selon S. Bonaventure*. Translated by Jacqueline Gréal. Paris: Éditions Franciscaines, 1970.

Gilson, Etienne. *The Philosophy of Saint Bonaventure*. Translated by Illtyd Tethowan and F. J. Sheed. New York: Sheed and Ward, 1938.

Hayes, Zachary. *Bonaventure: Mystical Writings*. New York: Crossroad, 1999.

———. *The Hidden Center: Spirituality and Speculative Christology in St. Bonaventure*. St. Bonaventure, New York: The Franciscan Institute, 1992.

Johnson, Timothy. *Iste pauper clamavit: Saint Bonaventure's Mendicant Theology of Prayer*. Vol. 390. European University Studies. Frankfurt am Main: Peter Lang, 1990.

Louth, Andrew. *The Origins of the Christian Mystical Tradition: From Plato to Denys*. Oxford: Clarendon, 1981.

Prentice, Robert P. *The Psychology of Love According to Bonaventure*. St. Bonaventure, New York: The Franciscan Institute, 1951.

Rout, Paul. *Francis and Bonaventure*. Ligouri, MO: Triumph Books, 1996.

Titles and Abbreviations of Bonaventure's Works

Apol. paup.	Apologia pauperum	1269	VIII
Brev.	Breviloquium	1256	V
Christus mag.	Sermo Christus unus omnium magister	1254–56	V
Coll. Jn	Collationes in Evangelium Joannis	1253–1254	VI
Comm. Eccl.	Commentarius in Evangelium Ecclesiastes	1253–1254	VI
Comm. Jn	Commentarius in Evangelium Joannis	1253–1254	VI
Comm. Lc	Commentarius in Evangelium Lucae	1248–1252	VII
Decem praec.	Collationes de decem praeceptis	1267	
De donis	Collationes de septem donis Spiritus Sancti	1268	
Hex.	Collationes in Hexaëmeron	1273	V
Itin.	Itinerarium Mentis in Deum	1259	V
Leg. maj.	Legenda maior sancti Francisci	1263	VIII
Leg. min.	Legenda minor sancti Francisci	1263	VIII
Lig. vit.	Lignum vitae	1260	VIII
M. Trin.	Quaestiones disputatae de mysterio Trinitatis	1253	V
Perf. ev.	Quaestiones disputatae de perfectione evangelica	1253	V
Perf. vit.	De perfectione vitae ad sorores	1259	V
Red. art.	De reductione artium ad theologiam	1253 or 1257	V
Sc. Chr.	Quaestiones disputatae De scientia Christi	1253	V
I, II, III, IV Sent.	Commentarius in I, II, III, IV librum Sententiarum	1250–56	I, II III,IV
Solil.	Soliloquium de quatuor mentalibus exercitiis	1259	VIII
Tripl. via	De triplici via	1259	VIII

Compiled by Jacques-Guy Bougerol *Lexique Saint Bonaventure*, 11–12 (Roman numerals refer to the critical edition of the *Opera Omnia* [Quaracchi 1882 - 1902]).

Glossary of Terms

Analogy

Refers to a likeness between two beings, which are essentially diverse. It describes a relationship between realities which are separated by the distance between finitude and infinite, as are God and creatures. Analogy is found in the order of internal arrangements and structure.

Congruity

Concerns the question of a fitting relation between a personal God and his creation. More specifically, it relates to fact that human beings are created as image of God and, specifically, as image of the Word of God by which there is an inner ordering of human nature to the mystery of the second divine person. Congruity underscores a principle of resemblance and analogy whereby the human person is immediately ordered to God and, thus, has the potency to receive the mystery of divine communication.

Contuition

In its specific sense, contuition implies an indirect knowledge of God in his effects. It is an intuitive type of knowledge of God whereby God is perceived in the created world without the aid of exterior senses. It is a sense of the presence of God together with the consciousness of created being, an awareness of the ontological presence of God attained in the consciousness of being. In the context of exemplary causality, it implies the awareness of simultaneity of form in the created thing and in the original or eternal exemplar.

Concupiscence

Expresses a desire, a movement of affective order or appetite toward something known and capable of giving satisfaction or pleasure. For Bonaventure, concupiscence is that which is associated with sin since it is an inordinate desire by which an object is sought for pleasure in itself. The terms "libido" and "cupidity" are sometimes used as synonyms, especially when the object of desire is sought for self-satisfaction or when the desire itself is immoderate.

Deiformity

Supreme end of all human persons, it is the stage at which the human person becomes a collaborator with God through participation in the divine life, manifesting the presence of God. Because the person is restored in the true knowledge and love of God through the memory, intellect and will, the person becomes "God-like" through the gift of grace. Restored in the image of God and wholly turned toward God, the person is a likeness or similitude of God and expresses this conformity through the power of love.

Desire

Enjoyment and possession of the most high good, that is, the enjoyment and possession, albeit imperfect, of God. It is a gift of divine grace, a gratuitous form of love that yearns to possess completely the beloved. Desire draws the soul upward in its ascent to God where, in union with Christ, the soul passes over in him to find its ultimate and total fulfillment in God.

Devotion

The orientation of the soul to God through the spiritual gifts of humility and piety. It is a habit of the soul by which grace enables the soul to be turned to God and to Christ through the raising up of one's mind and heart to God.

Ecstasy

A grace-filled experience by which intellectual knowledge of God is transcended and the soul enters into the mystical darkness of love. It is an affective state and the highest level of union with God that takes place in the innermost portion of the soul, the *apex mentis*. Although it is an affective experience of the will that goes beyond the intellect, ecstasy affords an experiential knowledge of God in which the soul enters into a union of love.

Exemplarism And Exemplar

Exemplarism is the doctrine of relations of expression between God and creatures. God is the exemplary cause of all things, because God in knowing himself expresses his most perfect idea, the *rationes* or the eternal patterns of all possible things. Everything that exists, therefore, is in some way related to God as a copy or imitation. Bonaventure distinguishes three different degrees of resemblance: the vestige, image and similitude. The examplar is the pattern or original model in whose likeness all things are made. It is the basis of imitation. Because the Word expresses the Father's ideas, the Word is the exemplar of all that exists.

Expression

Literally meaning "pressing outwards," expression corresponds to image and imitation. To imitate is to express. When the term image is applied to God, it denotes not only expression but the highest expression. Since God is supremely one, he finds his highest expression not in a multiplicity of images, but in one only, which is the most perfect reflecting likeness, the Son. In the Son, the Father expresses himself uniquely and definitely and in expressing himself, he expresses his whole power and his whole capacity.

Grace

A gift bestowed and infused directly by God. With grace and by means of grace, we receive the Holy Spirit, the uncreated gift of God given to us through the Word made flesh. Grace is also the gift by which the soul is perfected and transformed into the spouse of Christ, the daughter of the Father and the temple of the Holy Spirit. Finally, grace is a gift that cleanses, enlightens and perfects the soul; that vivifies, reforms, and strengthens it; that lifts it up, makes it like to God, and unites it with him. Sanctifying grace is that gift of grace by which the soul is conformed to God and is united to God.

Hierarchy

Referring to the principle of sacred order, hierarchy connotes a divine order, a knowledge and action of being assimilated to God. It is God-conformity which enables the soul to rise up through a divine influence of grace, that is, to become deiform or God-like. Since grace comes to us through Christ, it is the illumination of the soul in conformity to Christ. In union with Christ, who is the source of grace, the soul is illumined or "hierarchized," meaning that the soul, filled with grace, is sealed by the Holy Spirit so that, ultimately, the soul loves with the same charity as Christ.

Love

Supreme form of the good and the very essence of the Godhead, love belongs to the nature of God as self-diffusive goodness which is self-communicative. The basis of the three divine persons is predicated on the nature of God as love. On the human level, love is that act of the will whereby it unites through ardent longing to any of the three goods: the honest good, the useful good, and the pleasurable good. It is a union that results from the soul's going out of itself to unite itself with another object. Metaphysically, love belongs to the accidental order since love transforms the lover into the likeness of the beloved and not into the beloved him/her self.

Medium

The middle or center who stands between two extremes sharing the properties of both, and who communicates between them. The Word is the center of the Trinity because the Word is between one who produces and one who is produced. The Word is also center between God and creation and communicates between them.

Participation

Refers to the way creatures can share in or possess the life of God. It is a mode of possession in which what is possessed is received from another who is essentially different. In a proper sense, participation refers only to human beings since only they can consciously share in the life of God through grace.

Spiritual Senses

Inner senses of the spirit—touch, taste, sight, smell and hearing—by which the soul can perceive the presence of God. As spiritual gifts, they are the fruit of wisdom attained in union with Christ, and are integral to the contemplation of God. As eternal Word, God is seen and the harmony of the Word is heard; as incarnate Word, God's wisdom is tasted and his love is embraced; as inspired Word, God's fragrance is inhaled.

Synderesis

Innate natural gift of the will by which the will is oriented toward the good. Synderesis is in the highest part of the soul and is the primary impulse toward the good. It is a "weight" that stimulates the will toward what is good in the same way that the natural light stimulates the intellect toward what is true. It does not make itself part of our faculties of desire and action but it moves them, watches over them, directs them and corrects them as the natural light guides all the operations of our intellect.

Wisdom

Experiential knowledge of God deepened by love whereby charity renders the soul a divine similitude through the unitive power proper to love. As the fullness of love, it is an interior "tasting," or delighting in the divine. It delights in God as good in the interior of the soul and sees the right ordering of all things in the book of creation. As the uncreated and incarnate Word, Christ is the book of wisdom. Supreme wisdom is revealed in the cross of Jesus Christ.

Index

H

I

J

K

L